"Emilio Ramos's excellent little
unbreakable truth of the Holy
insights from God's servants, s
fruitful in practical application

"The cross is the center-point of history, the focus of God's redemptive
purposes, the pinnacle of God's sovereign self-glorification. Emilio Ramos proclaims the "word of the cross" boldly in his life and ministry, and
seeks to encourage us all to do so in this study of the crucifixion as the
soul of the gospel."

—James White
Director, Alpha and Omega Ministries

"Read this book and be set ablaze."

—Todd Friel
Host, Wretched TV and Radio

"His affection for the message of the cross shines brilliantly throughout
this wonderfully instructive and edifying examination of the crucifixion
and its role in the story of salvation. Every chapter is full of insight and
encouragement."

—Phil Johnson
Executive Director, Grace to You

"Few doctrines give us more comfort and strength than the news of what
Jesus Christ did on the cross to save His people. In "Crucified - The Soul
of the Gospel," Emilio Ramos not only delves deeply into this subject,
but he also manages to give us a rich appreciation of it without sacrificing
the simplicity of the Gospel."

—Lane Chaplin
Blogger, LaneChaplin.com

"Crucified exalts the glorious gospel of Jesus Christ. Every believer will
profit from reading this book. It is an absolute must-read."

—Mike Sarkissian
Author, *Before God, The Biblical Doctrine of Prayer*

CRUCIFIED:

The Soul of the Gospel

Emilio Ramos

A Publication of

REDGRACEMEDIA

www.redgracemedia.com

Scripture quotations taken from the New American Standard Bible®
(NASB), Copyright © 1960, 1962, 1963, 1968, 1971, 1972, 1973,
1975, 1977, 1995 by The Lockman Foundation
Used by permission. www.Lockman.org

ISBN: 978-0-9985939-0-6

To my daughter

Eden Joy

ACKNOWLEDGMENTS

There are so many people that I wish to thank for this project. A very special thanks to those who assisted in editing the document: my dear wife Trisha, Liz Ebert, Kristen Rasor, and Laura Moses. To John Manning, for taking the time to format the document for both print and digital platforms. To my church, Heritage Grace Community Church for giving me the opportunity to use my gift of preaching year after year. To all those who were thoughtful enough to pray for this book. Endeavoring to self-publish is a big decision for any author. I am thankful to Phil Johnson for encouraging me to pursue the path of self-publishing and for agreeing to do the foreword to Crucified. I am also grateful to Todd Friel and James White for their endorsement, their influence and friendship. Crucified reflects a deeply held belief that the cross-work of Jesus is the soul of the gospel. This is why Paul is unwilling to compromise its message and centrality in Christian thought. For those who share this cross-centered sentiment, thank you for your labor in the gospel.

TABLE OF CONTENTS

FOREWORD

No truth in all the universe is more important or more powerful than the gospel. It is the central message of the New Testament and the truth to which the Old Testament always pointed. Jesus Christ is the centerpiece of the story, of course, and the gospel is first and foremost the account of how He saves His people from their sins (Matthew 1:21). In short, the gospel announces that full atonement for sin was bought by the death of the sinless Son of God, and His resurrection certified that the payment rendered has been accepted. In other words, redemption from sin is provided for sinners at an infinite cost paid by God Himself; it is not something sinners must earn for themselves. Salvation—including full forgiveness for sin, a right standing before God, abundant life, and the eternal bliss of heaven—is freely given to those who confess and repent of their sins and trust Christ alone as Savior.

The apostle Paul used a distinctive shorthand expression to refer to the gospel. He called it "the word of the cross" (1 Corinthians 1:18). When he said, "We preach Christ crucified" (1:23), he was declaring his unshakable commitment to keeping the gospel at the center of his message. He described his ministry to the church at Corinth in these terms: "I decided to know nothing among you except Jesus Christ and him crucified" (2:2). That's because the message of the cross—the gospel—"is the power of God for salvation to everyone who believes" (Romans 1:16).

That very power changed Saul of Tarsus (a proud, cruel, zealous, and spiritually dead Pharisee) into Paul the apostle, the paragon of humility and godly patience. Before his conversion, he was the chief pharisaical inquisitor. He did evil to believers wherever he found them (Acts 9:13-14). But after his conversion, he himself suffered for Christ's sake. History records that he was finally martyred at the hands of Nero. In other words, from the time he met Christ on the road to Damascus until the end of his life, he endured the same kind of persecution and harassment he had once inflicted on others. But he wrote, "For the sake of Christ, then, I am content with weaknesses, insults, hardships, persecutions, and calamities" (2 Corinthians 12:10). This was a totally transformed person, thanks to Christ and the cross. No wonder he told the Galatian churches, "Far be it from me to boast except in the cross of our Lord Jesus Christ, by which the world has been crucified to me, and I to the world" (Galatians 6:15). And no wonder he devoted his life to bringing the gospel to others.

The apostle Paul's single-minded commitment to the gospel message has long resonated with me. I was converted in 1971 when, feeling the despair of human guilt, I picked up a Bible, opened it at random, and began to read. At the time, I was a spiritually disillusioned student, a casualty of modernist religion. A decade of Sunday-school instruction in a spiritually bankrupt, theologically liberal denomination had left me hopeless and hollow but not quite skeptical enough to abandon God completely. One sleepless night while pondering the direction my life seemed to be heading, I decided to do something I had never done seriously before: read the Bible.

I owned a Bible, but rarely used it. I would occasionally let it flop open at random, and then I would read just a verse or two. I would choose whatever random verse my eyes first fell on, reading it the same way I might view a fortune cookie or the daily horoscope in the newspaper. But my sense of spiritual poverty was so deep and oppressive that particular night I thought I would read an entire chapter. In the providence of God, my Bible fell open to the first page of 1 Corinthians, so I decided to read the entire epistle.

First Corinthians is not where the typical soul-winner would point a troubled teenager seeking the comforts of the gospel. It is an epistle to a dysfunctional church. It addresses a series of significant problems related to church polity, Christian living, marriage and divorce, order and authority, doctrine, and sanctification. Parts of it are very hard to understand without knowing something of the context. And the parts that are most understandable do not necessarily seem calculated to give hope to the hopeless or bring cheer to someone who is despondent.

Indeed, as I read 1 Corinthians that first time for myself, there was much that I did not understand, and at first I was more disturbed and discouraged than uplifted. But because Paul's ministry to the Corinthians was so deeply gospel-saturated, the central truths of the gospel became perfectly clear to me that night.

In the opening chapters of the epistle, for example, I learned that the talents and accomplishments I was most proud of were of no account in the reckoning of God: "For it is written, 'I will destroy the wisdom of the wise, and the discernment of the discerning I will thwart.' Where is the one who is wise? Where is the scribe? Where is the debater of this age? Has not God made foolish the wisdom of the world?" (1:19-20).

I thought it would make perfect sense to me if God said he hated the foolish things of this world. I could see why He would hate what is vile and unsophisticated. But as I read those opening chapters of 1 Corinthians, I was struck and deeply disturbed by the fact that God hated, not only, the rank sin in my life; He despised my righteous veneer even more.

Furthermore, if I wanted to be truly wise in God's eyes, I must be a fool in the eyes of the world: "Let no one deceive himself. If anyone among you thinks that he is wise in this age, let him become a fool that he may become wise" (3:18). God is clearly unimpressed with any human achievement: "God chose what is foolish in the world to shame the wise; God chose what is weak in the world to shame the strong; God chose what is low and despised in the world, even things that are not, to bring to nothing things that are, so that no human being might boast in the presence of God" (1:27-29). Suddenly, I began to feel very lost and sinful.

As a first-time reader, I naturally did not fully understand the weight and gravity of the problems Paul was addressing in Corinth. There was, for example, serious division in the Corinthian fellowship. Believers there were foolishly tolerating serious sin in their midst—up to and including one member of the church who was living in an incestuous relationship with his father's wife. Corporate gatherings in the Corinthian church were often chaotic—with drunkenness, gluttony, and competition over charismatic gifting. There was doctrinal confusion, including serious heresy. Someone in Corinth was evidently questioning even the resurrection of Christ. Women were challenging or defying the leadership of their husbands. Church members were suing one another in secular courts.

Some church planters would simply give up in despair and walk away. Not Paul. He poured his life into the people he was shepherding. He lovingly instructed them, rebuked them when necessary, served them however he could, encouraged them to persevere, and devoted his time and energy to their spiritual well-being. And he persisted at this task even when he himself was in chains, in prison, or under the threat of execution. In all of this, he continually brought them back to the gospel and showed them that's the starting place for every answer to every problem in the church. More than that, the gospel is where every problem that plagues all of humanity is ultimately resolved.

As I read 1 Corinthians, I was absorbing gospel truth. When Paul rebuked these young believers for arrogance and urged them "rather to mourn" in 5:2, I sensed a prodding in my own soul to repent. I knew I was as guilty as any Corinthian of sinful pride and spiritual rebellion, so every apostolic scolding aimed at that wayward church smote my heart as well. By the time I reached chapter 12, I knew beyond doubt that I was well and truly lost.

But then I began to notice what separates God's people from God's adversaries, and I began to find hope in the biblical summons to faith. I was largely mystified by 1 Corinthians 12:3 ("I want you to understand that no one speaking in the Spirit of God ever says 'Jesus is accursed!' and no one can say 'Jesus is Lord' except in the Holy Spirit."). But whatever else that verse meant, I understood that God sees no third option and no middle way between blaspheming Christ and honoring Him as Lord. That realization filled me with a desire to bow to the lordship of Christ and seek His mercy on my soul.

At the start of chapter 15, I encountered Paul's simple summary of gospel facts: "That Christ died for our sins in accordance with the Scriptures, that he was buried, that he was raised on the third day in accordance with the Scriptures" (vv. 3-4). And somehow, in a rudimentary sense, I began to understand for the first time the central truth of the gospel: that Christ had taken my place in death, and now I was entitled to stand by faith with Him in resurrection life.

That simple, flawed (but adequate) reading of 1 Corinthians gave me a dose of the gospel that totally transformed my values, my passions, and every aspect of my worldview. More than forty years later, I still love the gospel and it still seems as fresh and amazing to me as it did that night. There is no truth I love more.

And there is no more precious symbol of the gospel's true meaning than the cross—not the shape; not an emblem made into a piece of jewelry; not even the literal wooden cross-beams on which Jesus died, but the crucifixion itself—specifically, the work of atonement Jesus accomplished there. Remove that from the story and you have no gospel at all.

Emilio Ramos understands that, and he too loves the gospel. His affection for the message of the cross shines brilliantly throughout this wonderfully instructive and edifying examination of the crucifixion and its role in the story of salvation. Every chapter is full of insight and encouragement.

Emilio and his wife, Trisha, are two of the most earnest, faithful personal evangelists I have ever met, and once you have finished this book, I think you will appreciate why they are so passionate about sharing the good news with others. May that enthusiasm prove infectious, and may we never relinquish our passion for the gospel of Jesus Christ.

Phil Johnson
Executive Director, *Grace to You*

Dear Reader

Quite possibly, the most significant thing that you can dwell on during your life as a non-Christian is your death. Simply considering the absolute finality of that all-determining event is enough for the importance of this theme to present itself to you. At the very moment in which one passes from this life and this world and into the next, eternity will be forever fixed. I realize that only by the grace of God will you ever move out of the realm of contemplating religious things and experiencing what the Scriptures call being "born again." But if you would have any interest in Jesus Christ, using His words, "you must *be* born again" (Jn. 3.7), as it stands, life without Christ means that you stand estranged from God, you are at odds with God and there remains an infinite chasm of hostility between you and your Creator.

This book is the attempt to magnify how Jesus Christ bridges that gap and rescues sinners from perishing in their sinful condition. The Bible calls this the gospel—Christ crucified for sinners that He might bring us to God (1 Pet. 3.18). I realize that the world we live in today undermines one's desperate need for salvation at every turn. We are distracted by materialism, technology, television, entertainment, and news media. Yet, all of these sedative tools cannot take away the agony of a smitten conscience. It is only by personal faith and trust in Jesus Christ that our consciences can be cleansed and redeemed. The Bible is plain on the subject of salvation; we are sinners who have broken God's laws (e.g. the Ten Commandments), as such, we are in a miserable state.

If you would, God has placed us on red alert because we are headed for destruction in our sins. God would actually have you focus on two deaths, ours and Christ's. By focusing on your own death you may be awakened to seek salvation. By focusing on Christ's death you may be confident that you are gazing upon the only source of salvation. As you look at the cross, you will look upon God's Son, the Jewish Messiah, the Savior of the world, and the sacrifice which can take away your sins (Jn. 1.29).

The cross is God's greatest expression of His love for sinners. The Bible calls the cross a *curse* (Gal. 3.13), yet it is this curse-bearing cross that possesses all of the beauty of God's grace. Every aspect of the cross is grace. It was by God's own grace that He sent His Son to die for unworthy sinners, it was by grace that Jesus willfully laid down His life for sinners, and it is by grace that we are given the ability to partake in the work of the cross through faith in Jesus Christ. My prayer is that before you read *Crucified*, you would put the book down, and close with Christ. That you would personally turn from your sins, confess your sins and forsake them, turn to Christ in faith placing all of your hope upon His finished work on the cross. The thief on the cross next to Jesus did this very thing, and it was the crucified Christ who turned to Him and gave Him this unspeakable promise, "today you will be with Me in paradise" (Lk. 23.43).

Emilio Ramos

INTRODUCTION

I will never forget the time I was invited by a pastor friend of mine in a nearby Hispanic Baptist church, to attend one of their ordination ceremonies where several men were being appointed to the offices of elder and deacon. The most memorable moment for me came when a retired Baptist minister, who had pastored for several decades, stepped to the pulpit to address those being ordained. He must have been over eighty years old, his hair all grey now, his body looked frail and fragile, and he needed help standing and could not speak very clearly or very well. Yet, after giving a comment or two and congratulating the men for their introduction to the ministry, he roused himself to make one final exhortation (in Spanish of course) and with ascending intensity he reminded the men of one crucial and all-important focus for gospel centered ministry, "We must preach Christ"! "We must preach Christ"! "We must preach Christ"! The words rang out in that little church louder than what anyone else had said in that service. At the time I had just begun pastoring myself and took the exhortation as my own. This was a decision I had to determine to make for my ministry. Of course, this decision was all the more penetrating being rooted in Paul's own famous resolve, "For I determined to know nothing among you except Jesus Christ, and Him crucified" (1 Cor. 2.2).

The decision to preach Christ is a gutsy, risk taking, faith based mission. Once we have resolved, like the apostle Paul, to preach as our central evangelistic loci, Jesus of Nazareth crucified for sinners, we have put all our chips on Christ. But according to Paul, all other ground is sinking sand anyway (1 Cor. 2.2; Phil. 3.7-8). There is no foundation like the blood of Jesus. No other atonement can be afforded the sinner outside of the Lamb of God, no other substitution can be made for him, no other mediator can be found for man outside of the *theanthropic* man, Jesus

Christ (1 Tim. 2.5). Jesus is truly the hope of sinners (Rom. 5.1.5). He is the hope of the nations, and to be outside of God's redemptive promises is to be outside of the realm of saving hope, because all God's promises are summed up and understood to be affirmed in Him (2 Cor. 1.20; Eph. 1.10). Jesus did not spread His hands on the cross, nor shed His precious blood on the tree, or pour Himself out to death in order that His people would go groping for alternative messages than that of His scandalous cross-work. For Paul, to preach some other emphasis in evangelism was unthinkable because only through a cursed and crucified Messiah could we be saved from the curse ourselves (Gal. 3.13; 5.11). Where the Law demanded a curse, the cross demanded a pardon.

To recall another illustrative occasion, I was invited to speak to over a thousand students at a Baptist University where I preached on the need to stay faithful to preaching the Word of God in the ministry. Afterwards, I sat with a member of the faculty of the college where we began talking about missions and evangelism during lunch time. The faculty member shared with me that they had done extensive work among impoverished people groups where they would go in to provide humanitarian aid. As he was telling me the details of their mission, he said it dawned on him that it was things like digging wells for poverty stricken villages that would best communicate the gospel. In fact, he went so far as to say 'that *is* the gospel.' After listening to him go on about how he did not even have to say anything, and that the good works spoke for themselves, I gently interjected that the gospel was about the death, burial, and resurrection of Jesus Christ and that unless we talk about that, there could be no gospel at all (cf. 1 Cor. 15.3-4). Sadly, it seems that, for this faculty member, the message of Christ crucified was optional, something to be tacked on at the end of the day; after earning the right to be heard, once all of "the important things" had been taken care of first.

In such cases as this, what the church is communicating is that the cross is almost too obvious to focus on and too common to make the main business of evangelism and missionary activity. People think they need to look elsewhere to be relevant or to genuinely connect with people they are seeking to reach for Christ. So they proceed in becoming culturally focused, socially focused, and politically focused. Some think that perhaps acts of mercy or performing arts or music will connect the dots for people and cause them to want to follow Christ. When these sorts of assumptions are present, it does not take long before they replace the all-glorious slogan "Christ crucified" as the center of what they do with alternative mantras.

But as we will see, when the evangelist takes the name of Jesus Christ upon his lips, he takes to his tongue the great sum of all of God's saving activity, the great theme of all of redemptive history, and the maxim of Divine revelation itself. He is the Alpha and the Omega, the Beginning and the End, the Almighty. With His name, the evangelist evokes all of God's divine purposes and redemptive power. As we preach Christ, we speak of The Resurrection and The Life, The Light of the World, and The Prophet, Priest, and King of God's people. So then, we preach Christ simply because of His supremacy and sufficiency for the cause of the gospel and of bringing sinners into the Master's hall to dine with him and recline at His table in Holy Communion with Jesus, the great Shepherd, who lays down His life for the sheep.

When we come to the Bible, it may take years to discern the one sermon Scripture is preaching: tracing the inflections of biblical themes from Creation to Consummation results univocally in magnifying God's Son, whose person and work is the very theological thread which binds the book of God together. Jesus makes the Bible readable, intelligible, and transcendently genius. Every page is stained with His blood. Every chapter is either a shadow or a substance of Christological truth. In every epoch of redemptive history God is building either great anticipation or prophetic attestation concerning the Son of God.

With such a great emphasis upon Jesus Christ in the Bible, is it any wonder Paul would say he had one solitary God-exalting message, "Christ and Him crucified" (1 Cor. 2.2)? This was Paul's singular and all-consuming vaunt and glory, "May it never be that I would boast, except in the cross of our Lord Jesus Christ" (Gal. 6.14). For Paul, Jesus had become his purpose in life as well as his eschatological hope and reward, "For to me, to live is Christ and to die is gain" (Phil. 1.21; 3.14).

What is the design of this small volume? *Crucified* is written primarily with the evangelist in mind. However, all of God's people may benefit from becoming increasingly Christocentric and this is the overall aim of the book. We will endeavor to discover what motivated Paul to pen the eternal truths contained in 1 Cor. 2.2, "For I determined to know nothing among you except Jesus Christ, and Him crucified". We will also consider the missiological dimensions of the cross since all preaching is not limited to our local sphere of ministry here in America but must reach beyond our Jerusalem to the ends of the Earth. It is our position that the cross remains relevant, sufficient, and dynamic in the counter cultural mission of the Church and that based on Scripture itself. What gives rise to the preaching of the cross, namely, sin, sovereignty, and the great commission itself, reminds us that the only hope the world has lies in a crucified Christ— risen again for our justification (Rom. 4.25). We will also seek to inoculate ourselves with Paul's teaching of Christ crucified for the purpose of developing a healthy resistance to unhealthy, unbiblical, and ungodly methods of evangelism which often trend and move through the evangelical landscape.

The only safeguard against inadequate methods is, again, the cross itself and its many implications for sin and sinners. Every aspect of the gospel is concentric with the cross of Christ at the center. The cross makes the gospel make sense. Lastly, we will argue for what can be called a 'cross-centered-hermeneutic.' That is, we must grasp how the cross makes sense out of all of Scripture and consequently our sinful world as well. Our prayer is for believers to see that the cross-work of Christ gives life itself purpose, believer's their hope, and Scripture its loci. The cross is the redemptive link between the past, consisting of God's redemptive acts, history, and people; as well as supplying us with the goal of the future.

1

CRUCIFIED FOR HIS PEOPLE,
PREACHING ELECTION WITHOUT FEAR

The simple justification for speaking about election and evangelism is because Scripture does. Scripture is clear that God indeed has chosen a people to be His own possession (1 Pet. 2.9), that He is sovereign over the extent of His salvation (Jn. 17.2), and that the very atonement itself is unmistakably discriminatory in its design and purpose (Jn.10.15). Perhaps no other text draws the implication of election and salvation out with quite the same penetration as that of Acts 20.28, we Paul tells us that God was purchasing "the church…with His own blood". God's chosen ones are God's purchased ones (cf. Rev. 5.9).

Therefore, in order to truly witness to the great purpose of the cross is to speak about the *scope* of the cross. The cross was designed to accomplish a particular task, namely the salvation of God's people (Mt. 1.21). The cross is no sloppy affair. The cross is not a reaction. It is not a last minute cosmic scramble on God's behalf to see if anyone would turn to trust the saving work of His Son; instead, it flows directly out of the plan of redemption itself (Jn.17.1-5). God having purposed to save a people for Himself before the foundation of the world; prior to Moses, prior to Abraham, prior to Noah, and even prior to the fall of man in the garden. He had a purpose to glorify a people together with Himself in Heaven for everlasting joy by uniting them to His Son and His cross-work (cf. Eph. 1.4, Rom. 8.29-30). Therefore, God not only determined the objects of love, but also the instrumentality through which He would bring them into His possession, that is, through the cross-work of Christ.

God's plan of redemption was *designed* not conceded. God did not respond to sin, Satan, or man when He sent His Son to die for His people, it was always part of His great plan. Princeton Theologian Charles Hodge comments:

> "The Scriptures speak of an Economy of Redemption; the plan or purpose of God in relation to the salvation of men. They call it in reference to its full revelation at the time of the advent, the *οκονομία του πληρώματος των καιρων*, "The economy of the fullness of times." It is declared to be the plan of God in relation to his gathering into one harmonious body, all the objects of redemption, whether in heaven or earth, in Christ. Eph. 1:10. It is also called the *οκονομία του μυστηρίου*, the mysterious purpose or plan which had been hidden for ages in God, which it was the great design of the gospel to reveal, and which was intended to make known to principalities and powers, by the Church, the manifold wisdom of God. Eph. 3:9."[1]

God's plan was comprehensive in that it was designed to bring in God's people not simply to salvation, but into fellowship as a corporate group in the church. The doctrine of election was designed to inform demonic powers of the unfolding plan of God, which has overcome every satanic scheme to foil God's purpose (Col. 2.15). This satanic assault upon what would come to be known as *the mystery* (i.e. that which was previously hidden and now revealed to us in the gospel) has been under way since the fall of man when Satan deceived Eve from the simplicity of faith in God's Word (2 Cor. 11.3). Seeking to prohibit man's ability to produce the promised *seed*, Satan has been a murderer from the beginning. Still, God's purpose according to election continues (Rom. 9.11). Nothing can stop this plan from unfolding because God's plans are not subject to frustration (Ps. 115.3). The result is that the New Covenant minister, more than anyone, should be emboldened to be the means through which God will bring in His chosen flock.

Election makes evangelists brave, dependent, and humble

We can see the robust vitality that the doctrine of election had with great evangelists such as George Whitefield. During a correspondence with Wesley, who had expressed some objections regarding how election and evangelism would relate, Whitefield argued as follows:

---

[1]Charles Hodge, vol. 2, *Systematic Theology* (Oak Harbor, WA: Logos Research Systems, Inc., 1997), 313.

"—O dear Sir, what kind of reasoning—or rather sophistry—is this! Hath not God, who hath appointed salvation for a certain number, appointed also the preaching of the Word as a means to bring them to it? Does anyone hold election in any other sense? And if so, how is preaching needless to them that are elected, when the gospel is designated by God himself to be the power of God unto their eternal salvation? And since we know not who are elect and who reprobate, we are to preach promiscuously to all. For the Word may be useful, even to the non-elect, in restraining them from much wickedness and sin. However, it is enough to excite to the utmost diligence in preaching and hearing, when we consider that by these means, some, even as many as the Lord hath ordained to eternal life, shall certainly be quickened and enabled to believe. And who that attends, especially with reverence and care, can tell but he may be found of that happy number?"[2]

We can scan all of Whitefield's works for numerous examples demonstrating that he never shied away from declaring the sovereign counsel of God. Even in an open-air preaching setting where many are liable to be offended at the absolute sovereignty of God, Whitefield was unflinching in his commitment to the doctrines of grace. Instead of surveying the works of Whitefield (not the focus of the present volume) it would be beneficial to glean from Arnold Dallimore's beautiful expression and plea for more men like Whitefield. After spending decades steeped in the life, preaching, and ministry of Whitefield, Dallimore, who knew him better than most, expresses his personal desire to see God raise up a legacy to Whitefield of evangelists and preachers who will bear a similar mantel of gospel preaching; one that was "aglow with the great truths of the doctrines of grace":

"Yea… that we shall see the great Head of the Church once more bring into being His special instruments of revival, that He will again raise up unto Himself certain young men whom He many use in this glorious employ. And what manner of men will they be? Men mighty in the Scriptures, their lives dominated by a sense of the greatness, the majesty and holiness of God, and their minds and hearts aglow with the great truths of the doctrines of

[2]Whitefield, —Letter to Rev. John Wesley, in Journals, 575.

grace. They will be men who have learned what it is to die to self, to human aims and personal ambitions; men who are willing to be 'fools for Christ's sake', who will bear reproach and falsehood, who will labor and suffer, and whose supreme desire will be, not to gain earth's accolades, but to win the Master's approbation when they appear before His awesome judgment seat. They will be men who will preach with broken hearts and tear-filled eyes, and upon whose ministries God will grant an extraordinary effusion of the Holy Spirit, and who will witness 'signs and wonders following' in the transformation of multitudes of human lives."[3]

But did not Whitefield understand that election could circumvent evangelism? Certainly Whitefield knew that if God was sovereign in election then that would defeat the purpose of preaching altogether, right? However, despite this common misconception among Evangelicals, for Whitefield, the complete opposite was true. Whitefield saw election as Biblical and evangelistically necessary because the gospel was the means of bringing in God's chosen children from all the four winds of the earth (cf. Mt. 24.29-31). For this great unsurpassed evangelist, the doctrine of election was actually seen to be not the enemy of gospel preaching but its friend and ally.

This precise point also surfaced during the early upheavals of the Baptist movement. During the 17th and 18th century this precise issue of preaching and election came into focus. During the 18th century, Calvinism was facing off with Arminian, Socinian, and Antinomian preachers who were accusing Calvinists of slipping into Hyper-Calvinism (mostly held by John Gill 1697-1771) and saw election among other Calvinist tenants as antithetical to the mission of the church. However, the preaching of Andrew Fuller and the pioneer missionary activity of William Carey spoke directly against these accusations and actually established God's sovereignty and the Doctrines of Grace as the bedrock of true gospel preaching. In light of the developments of the Doctrines of Grace during these important centuries of Baptist life prior to the first Baptist Union (1812), Thomas Nettles rightly observes:

---

[3]Arnold A. Dallimore, George Whitefield, *The life and times of the great evangelist of the 18th century revival* (Edinburgh, UK/ Carlisle, PA: Banner of Truth Trust, 2009) vol.1, p.16.

"Nor did the rise of modern missions come as a result of shaking off the fetters of Calvinism, but instead issued as the necessary expression of it. This cannot be too strongly affirmed or stressed in the contemporary scene, where it is commonly believed that the Doctrines of Grace are the enemy of evangelism. Indeed, they are the enemy of systems and methods that thrive on reductionistic perversions of the gospel—but true evangelism has no dearer friend than these doctrines."[4]

The Puritan Baptists (among other Reformed churches) actually saw the Doctrines of Grace as a safeguard against veering off into heresy. Again Nettles (quoting Joseph Ivimey) points out the opinion and experience of Baptist pastors at a time when many in the General Baptists were slipping into gross theological compromise:

"Had our ministers in general manifested this strict adherence to the Calvinistic doctrines which Mr. Stennett did, instead of that spurious candour and moderation expressed by some others; there is no doubt but that many churches would have been preserved from the whirlpool of Socinianism, which has swallowed up some Particular Baptist Societies, and nearly all of those which at the end of the seventeenth century belonged to the General Baptists."[5]

Whitefield, Fuller, Carey and scores of others clearly establish not only the ability to believe in election while endeavoring to call the world to Christ, they were emboldened to do so. It was Spurgeon who declared, "I do not believe we can preach the gospel ... unless we preach the sovereignty of God in His dispensation of grace; nor unless we exalt the electing, unchangeable, eternal, immutable, conquering love of Jehovah; nor do I think we can preach the gospel unless we base it upon the special and particular redemption of His elect and chosen people which Christ wrought out upon the Cross."[6]

Christ's cross-work is discriminatory in nature. His cross is a special cross, it has a special purpose, it is not a role of the cosmic dice; God

---

[4]Thomas J. Nettles, *By His Grace and For His Glory* (Lake Charles, Louisiana: Cor Meum Tibi, 2002) p.31.

[5]Ibid. p.30.

[6]Charles H. Spurgeon, *Spurgeon's Autobiography*; Vol. I, Ch.XVI, p.172.

gambling with the life of His Son. The beauty of the cross consists of God's sovereign superintendence of every drop of blood, every act of righteousness His Son ever did, and every moment Jesus spent under the wrath of God was for the "many" God chose before the foundation of the world (Eph. 1.3-6). Long ago did Isaiah speak of the Messiah's particular redemption:

> **Isaiah 53:11–12** [11] "As a result of the anguish of His soul, He will see it and be satisfied; By His knowledge the Righteous One, My Servant, will *justify the many*, As He will bear their iniquities. [12] Therefore, I will allot Him a portion with the great, And He will divide the booty with the strong; Because He poured out Himself to death, And was numbered with the transgressors; Yet He Himself bore *the sin of many*, And interceded for the transgressors." (Emphasis mine).

Jesus, Calvin, and the Controversy of Election

From Augustine to Calvin and from Calvin to Spurgeon, the church has had an unmistakable tradition of exulting in the sovereignty of God. Yet, to suppose as so many erroneously do that teaching election and that preaching election originated with John Calvin is truly false. If we desire to preach like Jesus, to approach the whole subject of evangelism, we would do well to learn from the best example afforded to the believer in Jesus Himself. When we survey the biblical data we quickly find that Jesus, as the aforementioned men throughout the history of the church after Him, did not shy away from speaking about election and the sovereignty of God.

How often have we heard pastors tell their people not to bring up the subject of election while witnessing to their unsaved friends or during evangelistic outreaches, since that will only push people away? Many have concluded that it would be just better to avoid the subject of God's sovereignty all together. I distinctly remember reading one church manual for a particular denomination, which instructed the pastors of their churches not to preach election or the sovereignty of God, as it would only cause young believers to stumble and turn the non-believer away. This was the only reason the manual on distinctives gave to avoid preaching the doctrines of grace. The reality is that the doctrine of election like all other gospel truth, is based upon grace. In fact, when a person believes for their justification, God ordained that faith be the vehicle through which the righteousness of God in Christ comes. Why? Paul answers that question with God's grace, "For this reason it is by faith, in order that it may be in accordance with grace" (Rom. 4.16a). It was through the grace of faith that the promise of Abraham would come to all of the descendants of Abraham from "many nations" (Rom. 4.17). So too, in the ministry of Jesus and the apostles, election is preached because it accords with the grace of God. It stems from the grace of God and it results in the grace of God. Paul told the Ephesians:

> **Ephesians 1:3–6** [3] "Blessed be the God and Father of our Lord Jesus Christ, who has blessed us with every spiritual blessing in the heavenly places in Christ, [4] just as He chose us in Him before the foundation of the world, that we would be holy and blameless before Him. In love [5] He predestined us to adoption as sons through Jesus Christ to Himself, according to the kind intention of His will, [6] *to the praise of the glory of His grace*, which He freely bestowed on us in the Beloved" (Emphasis mine).

Far from being ashamed of God's electing love, Paul was proud to boast, literally exult in the reality of election, predestination, and adoption because it resulted in the glory of God alone. Jesus was fully aware of how the sovereign grace of God would redound to the glory of God and did not shy away from preaching it and teaching it to His disciples.

Admittedly, election and the sovereignty of God is not a popular topic today. Any time evangelists are asked about this Scriptural teaching they are tempted to shy away from the subject and many do. Jesus did no such thing. He was unafraid to declare that only some were of His sheep. Consider one passage in particular:

> **John 10:22–29** [22] "At that time the Feast of the Dedication took place at Jerusalem; [23] it was winter, and Jesus was walking in the temple in the portico of Solomon. [24] The Jews then gathered around Him, and were saying to Him, "How long will You keep us in suspense? If You are the Christ, tell us plainly." [25] Jesus answered them, "I told you, and you do not believe; the works that I do in My Father's name, these testify of Me. [26] *But you do not believe because you are not of My sheep.* [27] My sheep hear My voice, and I know them, and they follow Me; [28] and I give eternal

life to them, and they will never perish; and no one will snatch them out of My hand. [29] My Father, who has given them to Me, is greater than all; and no one is able to snatch them out of the Father's hand" (Emphasis mine).

If we notice from verses 22-24, Jesus is not in an intimate setting with His disciples behind closed doors where no one will hear his response to the Jews' unbelief, he is in public, "Jesus was walking in the temple in the portico of Solomon". Knowing their hearts, He does not give them what they want, straight talk about who He is (i.e. His Messianic identity). Instead, Jesus confronts their unbelief. Had they believed in the "works" that He had done in the Father's name, they would have understood Him to be the Son of God, which was itself a Messianic title. If ever there was an opportunity for Jesus to avoid the subject of election it would have been now. They were rejecting Him. They were in unbelief and thus were fully responsible for their own sin. But Jesus, probably to the amazement of His disciples, does not hesitate to supply the reason behind their unbelief, "But you do not believe because you are not of My sheep" (v.26). Too often this verse is tampered with and flipped upside down and read backwards so that people come away thinking that what Jesus actually said was, 'the reason you are not My sheep is because *you do not believe*'. But the passage is unmistakably predestinarian. Jesus is not explaining the reason why they do not belong to His sheep so that their unbelief has caused them not to enter into the number of Jesus' sheepfold, but rather, the number of the sheepfold, we could say, is the reason they will not believe. The number of God's sheep having already been determined, excludes all those who are not His sheep from entering the flock. As D.A. Carson was careful to observe the true meaning of the exegesis here:

> "The predestinarian note ensures that even their massive unbelief is not surprising: it is to be expected, and falls under the umbrella of God's sovereignty".[7]

We should also be careful to note that this 'predestinarian' interpretation of the text in no way undoes the responsibility man bears for His willful rejection of Jesus Christ· There are many passages that present the

---

[7]D. A. Carson, *The Pillar New Testament Commentary, The Gospel According to John.* (Grand Rapids: Eerdmans, 1991) p.393.

fine tension between God's sovereignty in ordaining all things that come to pass, and yet holding man fully accountable for his actions:

> **Acts 2:22–23** [22] "Men of Israel, listen to these words: Jesus the Nazarene, a man attested to you by God with miracles and wonders and signs which God performed through Him in your midst, just as you yourselves know— [23] this Man, delivered over by the predetermined plan and foreknowledge of God, you nailed to a cross by the hands of godless men and put Him to death."

> **Acts 4:27–28** [27] "For truly in this city there were gathered together against Your holy servant Jesus, whom You anointed, both Herod and Pontius Pilate, along with the Gentiles and the peoples of Israel, [28] to do whatever Your hand and Your purpose predestined to occur."

The controversy over election does not originate with Calvin, Luther, or any of the Reformers of the 16th century. or the fathers of the early centuries. It begins with *Scripture*, and the ministry and teachings of Jesus are no exception. James Montgomery Boice points us to this very truth when he commented, "The doctrines known as Calvinism are not something that emerged late in church history, but rather are that which takes its origins in the teachings of Jesus".[8]

As the Savior of the world, Jesus always saw His life saving mission in connection with this controversial doctrine. This doctrine will no doubt upset both believers and unbelievers alike. It may upset and split churches, cause evangelistic ministries to compromise or weaken their theology and message, cause a person to shrink back from declaring the whole counsel of God out of the fear of man and how people may respond to the Bible, it may harden the unbeliever in his/her sin; but it will also make one brave with the confidence that God has His elect and the gospel is the means to bring them in. In fact, the gospel *will* bring them in (cf. Mt. 24.14).

When election, properly understood, grabs a hold of the believer, evangelism will be done with a new found confidence that "salvation is of

---

[8]James Montgomery Boice, *The Gospel of John, Vol. 3: Those Who Received Him, John 9-12* (Grand Rapids: Baker Books 1999) p.778.

the Lord" (Jonah 2.9). It will open up new vistas of the cross. When we see that God's sovereign design of salvation in election has everything to do with the cross, it will bring all of God's redemptive actions together in a cross-centered fashion. J.I. Packer explains:

> "It cannot be over-emphasized that we have not seen the full meaning of the cross till we have seen it as the centre of the gospel, flanked on the one hand by total inability and unconditional election and on the other by irresistible grace and final preservation."[9]

Another aspect of preaching and knowing the doctrine of election is the sanctifying effect it has on the believer. When we grasp the truth that it is God's prerogative not only to elect but also to convert the soul, we will humbly come trembling to the goodness of our God for His saving mercy (Hos. 3.5). Jesus taught His disciples that they were utterly dependent upon God's mercy for salvation. Consider the following controversial passages, which again, were spoken in a public setting:

> **John 6:37–40** [37] "All that the Father gives Me will come to Me, and the one who comes to Me I will certainly not cast out. [38] For I have come down from heaven, not to do My own will, but the will of Him who sent Me. [39] This is the will of Him who sent Me, that of all that He has given Me I lose nothing, but raise it up on the last day. [40] For this is the will of My Father, that everyone who beholds the Son and believes in Him will have eternal life, and I Myself will raise him up on the last day."

> **John 6:44** [44] "No one can come to Me unless the Father who sent Me draws him; and I will raise him up on the last day."

The apostle John has often been called 'the apostle of sovereignty' precisely because of passages like these. However, let us never forget that it was the Lord Jesus Christ Himself that spoke these weighty words which John records. Again, the unmistakable thrust of this text is upon the sovereignty of God in salvation. The passage is a theological masterpiece. Here we get a further glimpse into God's plan of redemption. The components in the text imply that God, at some point, presumably in

---

[9] J.I. Packer, "Introductory Essay," in John Owen, *The Death of Death in the Death of Christ.* (Banner of Truth Trust 2002) p.15.

eternity past, chose to *give* to the Son *all* who *will come* to the Son (i.e. for salvation[10]) and would be *raised up* on *the last day* (i.e. the resurrection). This passage shows God's eternal purpose to save for Himself a special group of people out of all the nations of the earth (cf. Rev. 5.9) by "drawing" them to the Son for final eschatological glory. This sovereign plan could not be clearer. In his first volume entitled, *Foundations of Grace*, Steven Lawson draws out the same basic implications from these verses:

> "Jesus taught that before time began, God chose a vast number of individual sinners for salvation. He then gave these elect sinners to Christ to be His people. They were a love gift from the Father, a people who would worship the Son forever. Throughout the gospel of John, Jesus refers to these elect ones by the words "those whom the Father has given me" or similar terms (6:37, 39; 10:29; 17:2, 6, 9, 24). These are the same ones Christ chose for Himself when he came to earth. Because he is enslaved to sin, man cannot exercise his will to choose Christ. The sovereign choice of God both precedes and produces man's choice of Him. God's choice is the determinative factor that effects the saving faith of all believers."[11]

Thus the doctrine of election asserts that God chose men *in Christ* when God in His redemptive purposes decreed the plan of glorifying His triune deity through the work of the Son who would die for those whom God chose (Jn. 10.15). Only in the mysterious counsels of God's eternal mind does such a doctrine find its final explanation (Rom. 11.33-36). Yet Scripture is clear that this is God's purpose in Christ. This is why Jesus was unashamed to speak of God's sovereign grace because, regardless of how it would offend man, it would glorify God (Mt. 11.25-27).

The rest of Scripture supports not only the doctrine of election, its connections to the cross, but also its impetus for evangelism. When Elijah became discouraged in his prophetic ministry thinking everyone had

---

[10]In the gospel of John, the term *come* is often synonymous with *believing* in Christ for salvation (cf. John 6.36-40; see also, Mt. 11.28). The same would be true of John's of the terms *eating* and *drinking* (John 6.51-58). John's point is internalizing the Son of God by faith.

[11]Steven J. Lawson, *Foundations of Grace, A Long Line of Godly Men.* (Lake Mary, FL: Reformation Trust 2006) vol. 1, p. 278.

apostatized, God encouraged Him with election, "Yet I have reserved seven thousand in Israel, all whose knees have not bowed to Baal, and every mouth that has not kissed him." (1 Ki. 19.18) (NKJV). Subsequently, the prophet Elisha could also confidently continue with his ministry precisely because God had *reserved* for Himself seven thousand men that would not apostatized into Baalism, men who were kept by the power of God.

Jesus' entire ministry was in total harmony and under the guidance of God's sovereign will. For example, Jesus intentionally went into Samaria knowing He "had to pass though Samaria" because He had a divine appointment with a woman at a well, but more importantly because God's people were there, "many of the Samaritans believed in Him", again "Many more believed because of His word" (John 4.4, 39, 41). When Jesus chose His twelve disciples He displayed a perfect knowledge of God's sovereignty with regard to election saying, "... Did I Myself not choose you, the twelve, and yet one of you is a devil?" Now He meant Judas the son of Simon Iscariot, for he, one of the twelve, was going to betray Him." (Jn. 6.70-71). This passage makes it abundantly clear that Jesus was not simply referring to the disciple's calling or ministry, but to their salvation. He had perfect knowledge of Judas' unbelief because Judas was not elect. From the beginning of Jesus' ministry with the twelve, Jesus was sustaining the faith of the disciples, preserving them that they would not abandon the faith (cf. Lk. 22.31-32). Yet, with respect to the apostasy of Judas, Jesus was not surprised by his sin since even Judas' unbelief was sovereignly ordained by God being attested to by the Scriptures, "While I was with them, I was keeping them in Your name which You have given Me; and I guarded them and not one of them perished but the son of perdition, so that the Scripture would be fulfilled" (Jn.17.12, cf. Ps. 41.9).

During the ministry of Paul the apostle, we can also see this same type of confidence, humility, and dependence on the absolute sovereignty of God that characterized other individuals in the Bible. Luke gives the apostolic perspective on evangelism and conversion when he records Paul's first missionary journey. Paul and Barnabas were preaching to hostile Jewish audiences in the city of Pisidian Antioch, which is in the region of Galatia, where they preached on the Sabbath for several weeks seeking to preach Christ to Jewish communities first; as was Paul's custom (cf. Acts 17.1-2). Although Paul and Barnabas initially were tolerated by the Jewish community, their preaching became such a sensation of sorts that at one point, "nearly the whole city assembled to hear the word of the Lord" (Acts 13.44). But the Jewish leaders became so indignant and ultimately forced them out of town driving them to Iconium (Acts 13.51). Although Paul and Barnabas were seemingly rejected by the Jews, the Gentiles, which were in the region, who were chosen by God received salvation in sovereign fulfillment of the Scriptures:

> **Acts 13:46–48** [46] "Paul and Barnabas spoke out boldly and said, "It was necessary that the word of God be spoken to you first; since you repudiate it and judge yourselves unworthy of eternal life, behold, we are turning to the Gentiles. [47] "For so the Lord has commanded us, 'I have placed You as a light for the Gentiles, That You may bring salvation to the end of the earth.'" [48] When the Gentiles heard this, they began rejoicing and glorifying the word of the Lord; and as many as had been *appointed* to eternal life believed"[12] (Emphasis mine).

The predestinarian force of this passage surrounds the word, *appointed* ($\tau\acute{\alpha}\sigma\sigma\omega$) . This simply refers to God bringing something about, to arrange and put things into place as He sees fit. Darrell Bock brings out the unmistakable meaning of the text here:

> "Here it [*appointed*, $\tau\acute{\alpha}\sigma\sigma\omega$] refers to Gods' sovereign work over salvation, where God has assigned those who come to eternal life… The passive voice indicates that God does the assigning. It is as strong a passage on God's sovereignty as anywhere in Luke-Acts and has OT and Jewish roots… Just as God was the major active agent in the events of Israel's history earlier in the speech, so He is the active agent in bringing Gentiles to Himself."[13]

At this point it would be totally unduly to insert any activity, merit, goodness, freeness, or ability in those who believed as if that were the cause of God's choice, it is not. This is another place then where the free grace of God's electing love humbles us. It cripples us with respect to any works which can be deemed meritorious in any way whatsoever. Calvin commenting on this very passage, calls this, "the free adoption of God", said:

---

[12] Italics mine.

[13] Darrell L. Bock, *Baker Exegetical Commentary of the New Testament, Acts.* (Grand Rapids: Baker 2007) p.465. Brackets mine.

"For it is a ridiculous cavil to refer this unto the affection of those which believed, as if those received the gospel whose minds were well-disposed. For this ordaining must be understood of the eternal counsel of God alone. Neither doth Luke say that they were ordained unto faith, but unto life; because the Lord doth predestinate his unto the inheritance of eternal life. And this place teacheth that faith dependeth upon God's election… No marvel, therefore, if all do not receive the gospel; because, though our heavenly Father inviteth all men unto the faith by the external vice of man, yet doth he not call effectually by his Spirit any save those whom he hath determined to save. Now if God's election, whereby he ordaineth us unto life, be the cause of faith and salvation there remaineth nothing for worthiness or merits."[14]

The inspired writer in this instance was Luke, but no doubt Paul too was emboldened and humbled by God's sovereign choice. Paul labored under this all important premise; that God had His elect and that he could be the means through which they might be saved as he faithfully preached Christ crucified. This is more than clear from Paul's second letter to Timothy his young protégé, "Therefore I endure everything for the sake of the elect, that they also may obtain the salvation that is in Christ Jesus with eternal glory" (2 Tim. 2:10 ESV). A similar word is given to another young disciple of Paul, Titus: "Paul, a bond-servant of God and an apostle of Jesus Christ, for the faith of those chosen of God…" (Tit 1.1). This reality produced the deepest humility in Paul. He knew salvation belonged to our God and that he was expendable in the service of the Master (Acts 9.15; 17.25). At the same time it produced an indomitable confidence in Paul as an evangelist and missionary who was absolutely certain that his preaching was not in vain because God had chosen men and women who would be irresistibly drawn to faith in Christ by the preaching of the gospel. Had salvation been left to mere fate or chance or the willingness of man to believe in the gospel, Paul would have been dominated by a sense of unbearable doubt as to the effectiveness of preaching the cross.

Election and Preaching Christ Crucified

The cross is a prism of theological underpinnings. In the Bible we can say that the cross is the high point of revelation, the apex of redemptive

---

[14]John Calvin, *Calvin's Commentaries*. (Grand Rapids: Baker, 2005) Vol. XVIII, p.555-556.

activity, the zenith of salvation, and the centerpiece of the Christian message. Evangelism is the good news about a horrible event which transpired in human history where God's Son was cursed. Election is but one inflection of God's sovereign grace. Yet without a proper understanding of this essential doctrine, the whole design of the cross looses its Biblical symmetry (Rom. 9.11). Is it any wonder then that the more worldly the church has become the less sacred the cross with all of its theological implications appears in her preaching and evangelistic message? The current state of preaching certainly needs a good dose of God's sovereign grace. In a church culture where man has become the center, election has become as repulsive as the devil. Tell someone that the cross was designed to save only those whom God had chosen "in Christ" before the foundation of the world and you are quickly to be deemed a religious quack by the world, a mean and heartless heresy hunter in the church, and an overly zealous student in the seminary classroom.

But if we are to preach Christ crucified and not ourselves we have no right to empty the cross of its many offenses (cf. 2 Cor. 4.5; Gal. 5.11; 6.12). If we preach Christ crucified without fear we will preach for an audience of One. This is not to mean however that people engaged in evangelism begin or end with election as if we preach *election*—we do not! We preach *Christ* not election, we preach *Christ* not predestination, and we preach *Christ* not the sovereignty of God. Yet, when we preach Christ we do it with the full knowledge that God is sovereign and that Christ died for the sins of *His* people (Mt. 1.21), that His atoning work does not propitiate the sins of the world with no *exceptions* whatsoever (e.g. universalism), but rather no *distinctions* (Gal. 3.28; 1 Jn. 2.2). This, after all, is John's final word on salvation, namely that Jesus does not save everyone through what He did on the cross; He does not redeem without exception, but without distinction:

> **Revelation 5:9** [9] "And they sang a new song, saying, "Worthy are You to take the book and to break its seals; for You were slain, and purchased for God with Your blood men from every tribe and tongue and people and nation."[15]

---

[15]The use of the preposition here is crucial. The preposition "*ek*" (ἐκ) meaning "out of, from" governs all four groups so that we could render the syntax, "out of every tribe, and out of every tongue, and out of every people, and out of every nation" (ἐκ πάσης φυλῆς καὶ γλώσσης καὶ λαοῦ καὶ ἔθνους).

It is abundantly clear from this passage out of Revelation that Christ was *slain* and *purchased* certain men/people with His *blood* choosing them *from* (ἐκ) all of the tribes, tongues, people, nations of the earth. Although John's teaching on Christ's redemption is clear, nevertheless, the message of a limited salvation will continue to offend both the world and some in the church and when it does we must preach election without fear. We are reminded that regardless of how contemporary, relevant, tolerant, therapeutic, innocuous, passive, and gentle we preach the cross, the world will nevertheless deem the *true* cross *foolishness* (1 Cor. 1.18). So that, *wherever Christ is preached rightly he must remain forever intolerable to this Christ-diminishing world.*

The therapeutic-moralistic-deism[16] we hear so much about today, and worse so prominently proffered in our meeting places, houses of worship, churches, stages, and even pulpits, is a message eroding the Church's ability to treasure the preaching of Christ crucified for the sins of His people. This is largely in part because the Church has adopted the consumer model of church growth where success is measured above all by quantities; the number of attendees and the amount of tithes. These marketing and consumer driven goals, however, are training Christian men and women in such a way that they cannot contemplate anything dreadful or sobering or doctrinal for too long which is a disgrace not a virtue (1 Cor. 15. 34; Eph. 4.14; Heb. 5.11-14 cf. Prov. 1.22). Yet, this is the only real way the cross in all of its glory will be understood and appreciated. The only way that the church will truly praise God for His redemption in Christ is by contemplating, as Spurgeon put it, the "electing love of Jehovah." As philosophically challenging as the doctrine of election might be to us, it *does* reveal the glory of God's grace and is thus the fuel for true worship and praise (Ps. 147.19-20).[17]

At the heart of what makes this therapeutic trend in Evangelical churches so deadly is the inability for people to treasure the cross-work of Christ for what it is. Typically people in seeker sensitive churches may

---

[16]A phrase which Michael Horton traces to sociologist Christian Smith, see: Michael Horton, *Christless Christianity, The Alternative Gospel for the American Church.* (Grand Rapids: Baker, 2008) p.40.

[17]In a similar way, the psalmist is exulting in the Covenant Lord for having chosen to reveal His word (i.e. "ordinances/statutes") solely to the nation Israel. Likewise, Jesus is said to "reveal" the knowledge (apparently a salvific knowledge is in view) of the Father to those whom He desires (Mt. 11.27).

fall prey to the consumer driven church with nothing more than a life coach cheering them on with moralism and therapeutic psychology. Still, others may fall prey to mere emotionalism through an excess of charismatic activity, mysticism through quietism, or subjectivism through existentialism. While others may demand pure intellectualism, so that the cross is devoid of love and wrath. None of these options will do if we are to see the cross for what it is, Christ crucified for the sins of His people. Spurgeon once decried this form of dead intellectual orthodoxy:

> "Now, in these days there are some who would be glad if we would preach anything except Christ crucified! Perhaps the most dangerous among them are those who are continually crying out for intellectual preaching, by which they mean preaching which neither the heavens nor the preachers, themselves, can comprehend—the kind of preaching which has little or nothing to do with the Scripture and which requires a dictionary rather than a Bible to explain it!"[18]

Paul is so careful not to empty the cross of its power by reducing the cross to anything less than what it really is, the curse of God on His own Son for the sin of His own people, He *became a curse for us*, literally 'on *our* behalf' (*γενόμενος ὑπὲρ ἡμῶν κατάρα*) Galatians 3.13. Paul told the Corinthians that this salvation had been, "predestined before the ages to our glory" (1 Cor. 2.7). In every way, Paul steered away from the wisdom of the world, the cleverness of speech, the gimmicks, and the props of pretentious *underhanded* preaching which he deemed *disgraceful* so that the cross would not be devoid of its power (2 Cor. 4.2). Paul says, "For Christ did not send me to baptize but to preach the gospel, and not with words of eloquent wisdom, lest the cross of Christ be emptied of its power." (1 Cor. 1.17). The backbone of Paul's preaching therefore was not eloquence, it was not intellect, it was not morphology, and it was not scholarly minutia. Paul's confidence was that while his preaching may have been a *stumbling block* to the Jews and *foolishness* to the Gentiles, the reality that governed it all for Paul was *those who are perishing* and those *who are being saved* (1 Cor. 1.18, 22-23).

---

[18]C.H. Spurgeon, *Metropolitan Tabernacle Pulpit*, PREACHING CHRIST CRUCIFIED NO. 3218.

The reality was that the preaching of the cross was what coverts the soul (1 Cor. 2.1-5), the preaching of Christ crucified was what would cut to the very soul of man's conscience (Acts 3.23) and deliver him from his Adamic guilt, pollution, and death sentence.[19] The reality is that no other type of preaching will suffice to honor and glorify God, either in evangelism or in sermons, but Christ crucified for the sins of His people (Mt. 1.21).

We should endeavor in all of our preaching to boast that Christ has died for "a people" and when people object concerning the design of the cross, complaining about why God would send His Son to save only some, we should immediately return with the marvelous reality that God would send His Son to save *anyone*, when indeed He was not obliged to do so.

We have seen that election and evangelism are not at odds, they are actually friends and allies because both come from the preaching of Christ crucified. Furthermore, election is found throughout Scripture, election emboldened the greatest of evangelists throughout the history of the church, more importantly it caused the individuals in Scripture to be brave, humble, and dependent, knowing that God has His people in every place (2 Cor. 2.14-16). The authors and preachers in Scripture knew that they were incapable of producing salvation though manipulation, gimmicks, altar calls, and any other easy-believism methodology one could employ. Because for them salvation was impossible, but because with God all things are possible, they remained utterly dependent on the mercy and grace of God to sovereignly move upon the hearts of the *Lydias* of the world for regenerate faith (Acts 16.14; Mt. 19.26; Mk. 10.27). Part of this dependence involves the reality that, aside from Christ Himself, every other person including the prophets, the apostles, and all evangelists after them simply do not know who the elect are.[20] This dependency is thus expressed through the universal call of the gospel which historical Calvinism in the tradition of Calvin, Luther, Spurgeon,

---

[19] See, *Convert: From Adam to Christ* (Alachua FL: Bridge-Logos, 2012).

[20] This of course does not mean that we may not have a general level of assurance concerning the believers around us so that we live our lives filled with suspicion as to each other's election. The apostle Paul went so far as to thank God for the Thessalonians precisely because he had this general level of assurance regarding God's "choice" of them (1 Thess. 1.4). In fact, Paul uses the very word meaning election (ἐκλογή) here. Yet in the ultimate sense, we are not privy to the identity of the elect, this general assurance coming only after conversion has taken place.

Edwards, and the Puritans believed. Jesus said, "many are called, but few are chosen" (Mt. 22.14). Our job is to call the many to repentance and faith, and it is God's job to save those who are chosen.

But it is in this general and effectual call of the gospel that preaching election without fear makes the most sense. If people are called and if they are "appointed" to eternal life, they will believe and the rest will be hardened (cf. Rom. 11.7). This is a work of divine sovereignty, we simply are not sufficient of ourselves for this great sovereign work—God alone gets the glory for what God alone can do. The cross is a sovereign cross, meaning that it will accomplish precisely the mission for which it was designed. The elect will obtain salvation through the cross, the non-elect will be hardened by it. Either the cross will be a sweet savor to the elect or it will reek of death to those that are unbelieving. The gospel will either be the power of God for salvation or foolishness to those who are perishing (1 Cor. 1.18). The cross is a prism of many colors with many implications and consequences. God's plan and purpose in election is bound to the cross because the cross is the means of accomplishing and procuring redemption for the elect.

In the course of reading *Crucified*, we will look deeper into the prism of the cross with all of the glorious shades and emphasis Scripture lays upon it. We end this chapter with Paul:

> **2 Corinthians 2:15–16** [15] "For we are a fragrance of Christ to God among those who are being saved and among those who are perishing; [16] to the one an aroma from death to death, to the other an aroma from life to life. And who is adequate for these things?"

2

CRUCIFIED FOR OUR TRANSGRESSIONS, MAKING SINNERS AWARE OF THEIR MISERY THROUGH THE CROSS

It is no simple task to talk about what Thomas Watson called, 'the mischief of sin' in a world that specializes in maximizing mischief and sin. The consequences of living in a post-modern, decadent, pornographic, materialistic, sports idolizing, slander laden politicizing world that trivializes just about everything in the world, is that sin itself undergoes a complete redefinition. Indeed, sin has been reduced to failures and mistakes, from adultery to affairs, from lying to misspeaking, from sexual deviancy to art, and from self-autonomy to self-esteem. In his *Christless Christianity*, Michael Horton has captured the vanishing of sin's viciousness in our day:

> "As we lose a sense of Gods' gravity, sin loses its reference point. No longer falling short of God's glory (Rom. 3.23), sin is now falling short of the glory of the self. Everything is under control quite well without Christ. God is still keeping score—but only of the *good* things that we do, and the stakes are not quite as high: No longer an issue of our place in the life to come, it's just a question of getting the best out of life here and now."[21]

In other words, Horton is saying that when we fail to tell people about the gravity of sin, we fail to tell them something about "God's gravity". This is why we must make men sensible of their misery. If Horton's analysis is correct, to undermine the severity of sin is also to strip man of his other-worldly-accountability before God. Because man has come to accept the humanistic standards of his fathers, what man himself makes of sin must be the only assize that counts in the end. However, this hu-

---

[21] Horton, *Christless Christianity*, p.73.

manistic approach is disastrously deceptive. It assumes that there is no Judge of all the earth when there is (Gen. 18.25), it assumes that man will continue to get away with his/her sin ad infinitum and never pay for the wrongs they have committed when they will (Lk. 12.20; Rom. 2.16); and worst of all, sin's deceitfulness reaches its most detrimental point, not just by searing the conscience of man, but by blinding man to his need for the only Savior available to him (Hos. 5.4). Although many sinners might be awakened to their sin like Agrippa (Acts 26.28), not many are alarmed like the Philippian jailor so that they cry out, 'What must I do to be saved' (Acts 16.30).

But of course the problem with the world today is that even admitting the need to be saved by a 'Savior' is not 'healthy'. Deeper still is the illusion of many people today who think they are 'self-savable'. Man employs therapeutic techniques of every kind in the attempt to deliver themselves from their sense of 'wrongness' or spiritual emptiness. Because of the erosion of sin as an anthropological reality, the moral foundations of conscience are further diminished. David Wells has pointed out the type of mindset now dominating modern man's assessment of sin as no longer being a matter of guilt but of 'shame':

> "In the psychiatric literature, as well as in the wider culture, the transition to the language of shame from that of guilt really signals the secularization of our moral life. What it suggests is that any moral discomfort, any inward pangs that are the result of our actions, should be construed as *relational* problems not moral ones. They should be resolved along the horizontal plane of psychological understanding rather than against the vertical realm of theological knowledge. It is we who will dissolve our own shame, not God. It is we who will do it by technique, for when all is said and done, what is awry is simply the way we are viewing ourselves."[22]

For these reasons, if we are to faithfully preach Christ to a lost world, we must awaken them to their *vertically* oriented sins and show them just how impotently lost they really are so that, by God's grace they will find themselves alarmed enough to cry out and believe on the Savior. No

---

[22]David F. Wells. *Losing Our Virtue, Why the Church Must Recover its Moral Vision*. (Grand Rapids: Eerdmans, 1999) p.140.

matter how ignorant or hardened to their sin people are, preaching Christ crucified necessitates that we call men to repentance nonetheless (Acts 17.30; 20.21; 26.20). This is not easy to do, however, considering that we are in the age where technological advancements seem to be producing the type of pragmatism which followed the Industrial Revolution. The question once again becomes, *can we* regardless of *should we*. Man has begun to think he can solve everything through technology, even 'sin'.

Recently, *PBS* put out a segment in their religion and ethics section on December 9th, 2011—*Originally published: August 20, 2010.* The segment focused on technology and human enhancement. They featured Ray Kurzweil, an American author, scientist, inventor and futurist who is making some fantastic claims about how technology will change humanity in the future. His claims are so amazing that it prompted billionaire Bill Gates to say, "… he is the best in the world at predicting the future". Kurzweil is not afraid to explore the biological possibilities through technology for what he calls "singularity" or "matching human intelligence", which he hopes will "push back human longevity":

> "This is a design of a robotic red blood cell. We are going to put these technologies inside us, blood-cell-size devices that will augment our immune system, make us a lot healthier, destroy disease and dramatically push back human longevity, go inside our brains and actually enable us to remember things better, solve problems more effectively. We are going to become a hybrid of machine and our biological heritage. In my mind, we are not going to be transcending our humanity. We are going to be transcending our biology."[23]

Correspondent Lucky Severson, who did the piece, suggests that Kurzweil is motivated by the desire to live "indefinitely." However much we may end up manipulating our health, longevity, and biology and despite the desire like Kurzweil "to live indefinitely", man will always suffer from a *Jeremiah 17.9 condition*, which no super cell or any other man made genetic manipulation will overcome, "The heart is more deceitful

---

[23]Kurzweil is an award winning author of several books including, *The Age of Intelligent Machines*: published in 1990; *The Age of Spiritual Machines*: published in 1998; and his latest, *The Singularity Is Near*: which was published in 2005. The present reference was based on the *PBS* interview with Ray Kurzweil here: (http://www.pbs.org/wnet/religion-andethics/episodes/august-20-2010/ethics-of-human-enhancement/6823/).

than all else And is desperately sick; Who can understand it?". This is the real condition man needs to awaken to and overcome, not cancer, not their immune system, and not the possibilities of longevity.

But how do we awaken and alarm modern man to his sin in such an all-trivializing culture that wearies itself in belittling religious language of every kind? What has God given us as a relevant tool or means of making men aware of their miserable condition before a holy God? And what role if any does the cross play in making men sensible of their sin?

"...Through the Law comes the knowledge of sin" **(Rom 3:20).**

To bring the knowledge of sin was once as simple as mentioning the word sin. People, it seems, had the Judeo-Christian background to connect the dots. But today's society is quite different. Go up to the average person on the street and ask them what sin is and you will get as many answers as the people you ask. Even among evangelistic Christians today, too much talk of sin, and you run the risk of being labeled Fundamentalist or condemnatory. The church however is ripe for a new wave of gospel preachers that are more afraid of God than man. Sometimes the church should look to the voices of the past, before being moved by the faddish trends of the present. One sample of an old voice is Jonathan Edwards (1703-1758). He understood the dire need to make men sensible of their sinful condition before a holy God. Perhaps it was the holiness of Edward's God that made preaching so earnestly about sin so logical. Speaking of the unbeliever, Edwards says:

> "They must be sensible that they are not worthy that God should
> have mercy on them. They who truly come to God for mer-
> cy, come as beggars, and not as creditors: they come for mere
> mercy, for sovereign grace, and not for any-thing that is due.
> Therefore, they must see that the misery under which they lie is
> justly brought upon them, and that the wrath to which they are
> exposed is justly threatened against them; and that they have de-
> served that God should be their enemy, and should continue to
> be their enemy. They must be sensible that it would be just with
> God to do as he hath threatened in his holy law, viz. make them
> the objects of his wrath and curse in hell to all eternity.– They
> who come to God for mercy in a right manner are not disposed
> to find fault with his severity; but they come in a sense of their

own utter unworthiness, as with ropes about their necks, and lying in the dust at the foot of mercy."[24]

Unworthy of mercy, lying in misery, and justly condemned under the wrath of God to be His objects of a curse in Hell to all eternity— Edwards saw all of this as a result of what God's holy law 'threatens'. In the same fashion, Paul the apostle saw that far from justifying us or saving us, *through the Law*, a person becomes aware of his/her sin and awakens to terror of divine retribution (Rom. 3. 5-8, 20). Despite what others were thinking in terms of the efficacy of the Law,[25] for Paul, he saw the Law as capable of producing— not righteousness, but sin. In fact, Paul would argue that "The Law came in so that the transgression would increase" (Rom. 5.20a). This however does not mean that the Law is the cause of sin, rather the opposite is actually true, "sin, taking opportunity through the commandment" (Rom. 7.8a).

While the Jews actually saw the Law as a means through which, if obeyed (Phil. 3.9), one could actually become righteous in the sight of God, Paul saw that the Law could cause only a further and further increase of sin given man's *flesh* ($\sigma \acute{\alpha} \rho \xi$) (i.e. man's unredeemed human nature). This of course was not to say that the Law itself was weak, inconsequential, or evil; Paul saw the Law as good (Rom. 7.7, 12), and the nature of the flesh as sinful (Rom. 7.21-24). Thus, the problem of the Law and Justification arose not on account of God's *holy and righteous* commandments, but because of man's inability to live up to the Law's demands.

Paul would go on later to elucidate the place which the Law held for believers, particularly dealing with evangelism:

1 Timothy 1:8–11 [8] "But we know that the Law is good, if one uses it lawfully, [9] realizing the fact that law is not made for a righteous person, but for those who are lawless and rebellious, for the ungodly and sinners, for the unholy and profane, for those who kill their fathers or mothers, for murderers [10] and immoral men and

---

[24]Jonathan Edwards, *Jonathan Edwards on Knowing Christ* (Edinburgh: Banner of Truth, 1997) p.268.

[25]See, Thomas Schreiner, *Baker Exegetical Commentary on the New Testament, Romans* (Grand Rapids: Baker, 1998) p.173. Schreiner points out that certain "sectors of Judaism" actually held out hope for human nature and the ability to overcome evil and thus obey the law. As Schreiner puts it, "Justification by law is ruled out because no one could keep what the law said".

homosexuals and kidnappers and liars and perjurers, and whatever else is contrary to sound teaching, [11] according to the glorious gospel of the blessed God, with which I have been entrusted."

We have no other standard by which we can specify to sinners as to why they are in such a miserable state before God than His Law. All New Testament references to the moral Law of God are often nothing more than implications of God's moral Law in the Decalogue (i.e. the Ten Commandments). As it pertains to the sins listed in Timothy above and as Paul states, "…and whatever else is contrary to sound teaching" (1.10b), meaning things not mentioned here which are simply variations and mutations of the sins mentioned in this vice list, only the Law of God will show man why these activities are wrong. These sins are crimes against Heaven, they are crimes against God and man; crimes which men must be made aware of if they are to awaken to their misery and their desperate need for salvation.

The theology of sin for Paul begins with Adam in the garden (Rom. 5.14; 1 Cor. 15.20f). Because of Adam's sin, man has been infected with a deadly condition, in effect, he is already "dead in trespasses and sins" (Eph. 2.1). Sin entered into the world through Adam and death through sin so that death is reigning even now (1 Cor. 15.22; Rom. 5.12-14). Part of making people aware of their plight is communicating who they are *in Adam*. Most people have long believed that Adam is simply a mythical figure with no real and practical relevance to their lives today. If we could but warn and educate the sinner of the reality that controls the universe is their position either *in Adam* or *in Christ* they would understand their need to get out of Adam and into Christ.[26]

God has given us His commandments for this very purpose. As Paul says, the Law is for the *lawless* and the *ungodly*. Paul told the Galatians, that prior to conversion, the Law was our "tutor to lead us to Christ" (Gal. 3.24a).[27] When we use the Law to make man sensible of his condemna-

---

[26] See, E. Ramos, *Convert, From Adam to Christ.* (Florida: Bridge-Logos, 2012).

[27] After conversion Paul argues that we are no longer under the "*tutor*" (παιδαγωγός) having now become heirs with Abraham "*according to the promise*" (και ἐπαγγελίαν). This however does not mean the Law has become useless for indeed, Paul said "*I delight in the law of God according to the inward man*" (NKJV). Some call this the Third Use of the Law, God's Law no longer being used as a means of trying to justify oneself, it now becomes a good and trustworthy guide by which we can obey and glorify God. For further explanation for the third use of the Law see, Robert L. Reymond, *A New Systematic Theology of the Christian Faith.* (Nashville: Nelson, 1998) p.770-771.

tion, in essence all that we are doing is informing the sinner of the specifics regarding a law already at work in their hearts. If we return to Romans we find Paul, earlier in the letter, consigning all men under sin (3.9, 19). On the Gentile's part, those *who have no Law*, God's Law is nevertheless at work in their hearts through the light of conscience:

> **Romans 2:14–15** [14] "For when Gentiles who do not have the Law do instinctively the things of the Law, these, not having the Law, are a law to themselves, [15] in that they show the work of the Law written in their hearts, their conscience bearing witness and their thoughts alternately accusing or else defending them."

We should notice very carefully where many have often made the mistake of thinking that Paul said 'God's *Law*' is written in the hearts of unbelievers, since Paul says nothing of the sort. Paul is not claiming that people devoid of Scripture actually have the Ten Commandments written on their hearts. Paul is careful to specify that it is the "*work* of the Law" (τὸ ἔργον τοῦ νόμου) which is at work in their heart. The phrase, "the work of the Law" is best seen as a parallel of what Paul says in v.14, "the things of the Law" (τὰ τοῦ νόμου). This is an important distinction because only believers have God's *Law* written in their hearts in fulfillment of the New Covenant prophecies made by the Prophets (e.g. Jer. 31.33).

When God's Law is written in our hearts, we love to do God's will, we declare with the Psalmist, "I delight to do Your will, O my God; Your Law is within my heart" (Ps. 40.8). Therefore, when the Law of the Lord is at work in the heart, it is only for conviction of sin, righteousness, and judgment and not for pleasing God because that would imply that they know God and are in covenant relationship with God (cf. Jn.16.8). Paul makes this explicitly clear when he speaks of the unbeliever who is still under the Adamic nature which he calls, *the flesh*, "because the mind set on the flesh is hostile toward God; for it does not subject itself to the law of God, for it is not even able to do so, and those who are in the flesh cannot please God" (Rom. 8.7-8).

God does not save man through His Law, and certainly not by whatever measure of conscience or light the natural man has prior to salvation, or else what would be the need to preach Christ crucified (Rom. 10.17). Although common grace may be extended to all men, yet, no man is ever brought to saving faith through God's common grace. A *greater grace* (μείζονα...χάριν) is needed for a person to actually come to a saving knowledge of Christ, that is, the grace extended to him in the gospel.

The Law is the precursor to the gospel. God's law gives man a definite reference point for understanding their sin vertically. God's law, in a sense, legitimizes man's sin, it makes sin personal not abstract, real not theoretical, religious not behavioral, and rational not superstitious. To show the serious nature of sin, the great theologians of the church have spent great amounts of energy writing extensive volumes on the doctrine of sin. Herman Bavink (1854-1921) points out the truth of sin when he said, "…sin is never an arbitrary matter, merely a whimsical displeasure of a jealous God. Sin is knowingly breaking God's command and flows from a heart that rebels against God."[28] It is the heart of every criminal to want to make excuses for their offenses. The Law makes the sin inexcusable, Paul insists, "… they are without excuse" (Rom. 2.1, 17f).

The Law makes the sin a matter of righteousness. When people break God's laws it is not that they are merely being irresponsible, but rather they are being irreligious or more specifically, lawless (1 Tim. 1.9). Regardless if a person is atheistic, agnostic, skeptical or stoical; seeing sin in this way makes it a matter of God versus man. The sinner has this innate knowledge within him already but through sin and through self-deception, man suppresses the truth he already knows about God. Showing that sin is deliberate and voluntary makes people accountable and inexcusable to the things they already has a basic knowledge of (Rom. 1.18f).

The Law also provides man with a proper Creator/creature distinction from the outset. When we speak of God's Laws we are immediately implying that there is a Law Giver, a Judge, and a judgment. Thus, through the Law, man is made cognizant of his creatureliness, that is, that he is not the Creator, but the creature and thus under the sovereign rule of his Creator. God demonstrated His Sovereign authority in the garden when He gave Adam a very clear command, a Law, "The Lord God commanded the man, saying, "From any tree of the garden you may eat freely; but from the tree of the knowledge of good and evil you shall not eat, for in the day that you eat from it you will surely die" (Gen. 2.16-17). Adam understood the Creator/creature distinction more clearly within

---

[28]Herman Bavink, Reformed Dogmatics (Grand Rapids: Baker, 2006) vol. 3, p.126.

the context of God's authoritative Law. So too, the descendants of Adam, (i.e. his posterity), will become more aware of their accountability before a Sovereign and all-just God through the hearing of His commandments.

As we will see below, this is not a complete picture however; man is not simply to know God through the Law. As it pertains to salvation, the Law cannot save, it cannot convert, it cannot produce life; in fact, it can only kill. Taking opportunity upon the weakness of man's flesh, the Law can only cause the unbeliever's sin to thrive, tend towards further sin, and increase (Rom. 5.20). Paul explains:

> **Romans 7:7–11** [7] "What shall we say then? Is the Law sin? May it never be! On the contrary, I would not have come to know sin except through the Law; for I would not have known about coveting if the Law had not said, "You shall not covet." [8] But sin, taking opportunity through the commandment, produced in me coveting of every kind; for apart from the Law sin is dead. [9] I was once alive apart from the Law; but when the commandment came, sin became alive and I died; [10] and this commandment, which was to result in life, proved to result in death for me; [11] for sin, taking an opportunity through the commandment, deceived me and through it killed me."

"...The wages of sin is death" (Rom. 6.23).

Before considering the saving aspects of the cross, man must be made sensible of sin both in its reality and consequence. Therefore, to use the Law to bring the knowledge of sin does not stop at the *fact* of sin, but must continue on into the *consequences* of sin. Compounding the problem today is the fact that man is now being told he may know nothing of the life to come or even that there is a life to come. We live in an era of radical skepticism, a skepticism that is not easily overcome by mere religious talk. Our society has conditioned its citizens to be skeptical for good or for bad. It was Carl F. Henry that pointed out so lucidly that our society has created a deep-seated distrust for verbal communication, especially due to the influence of media and television:

> "A *Newsweek* survey (Aug. 16, 1971, p. 9) shows marked public disbelief of television commercials: even "as early as the second grade, children indicate 'concrete distrust of commercials, often

based on experience with advertised product' "; "by the fourth grade they have 'distrust for specific commercials and "tricky" elements of commercials' "; and "by sixth grade they show 'global distrust of all commercials except public service announcements… The breakdown of confidence in verbal communication is a feature of our times.' "[29]

In other words, propositional truth of all sorts has suffered a great affliction at the hands of our commercialization driven generation. The results are thus disastrous and the effects show up everywhere. If this sort of breakdown in verbal propositional truth was a feature in Henry's day, decades ago, what is it now?

Carl Henry went to be with the Lord on Dec. 7th 2003, but the problems he foresaw remain with us today. I know this to be true because of our church's outreach on college campuses. The university is one of the best places to gauge the mindset of young Americans today. On these campuses, postmodernism reigns supreme in the minds of the student body. Every truth claim is questioned, every biblical event and scriptural teaching is challenged and often mocked; the truth of the gospel itself is subject to gross and foolish suspicion. Sadly, there is a sinister reality in all of this, for in undermining the authority and teachings of Scripture, people forfeit their only hope of escaping their blindness and vicious skepticism in the first place. Furthermore, the consequences of their sins are likewise trivialized and discarded, so that they see no need to believe saviors, gods, or sacred texts of any sort. Because many young people today do not 'feel' the need to be saved, a conviction informed by today's militant atheism and radical skepticism, talk of a Savior is a sign of mental weakness and low self-esteem.

Regardless of a person's hardened condition or recalcitrant resistance, the consequence of sin is far too grave to simply go unsaid. Every true and faithful gospel presentation should and must entail the consequences of sin, as well as the reality of sin, the origin of sin, and the presence of sin.[30]

---

[29]Carl Ferdinand Howard Henry, *God, Revelation, and Authority* (Wheaton, Ill.: Crossway Books, 1999) vol. 1, p.25.

[30]Grudem lists the various elements essential to a faithful gospel presentation, see Wayne Grudem, *Systematic Theology* (Grand Rapids: Zondervan, 1994) p.694f. The four essential components are: The guilt of sinners (Rom. 3.23); the penalty for committing sin (Rom. 6.23); the payment Christ made for sin and sinner (Rom. 5.8); and an invitation for sinners repent and believe (Mk. 1.15).

However happy people seem apart from the knowledge of sin and its consequences, we should never overlook the reality of the wrath of God, the sobering truth of the eternality of Hell, and the hopeless nature of the unbeliever's worldview. Neither should we underemphasize the crimes which people have committed by breaking God's laws. Man has to see himself as lost in his sin if he is ever to be found by God's grace (Lk. 18.9-14).

Finally, we should never give in to the popular temptation to preach our own consequences for sin rather than the Bible's. If we stop at death we have not preached an accurate message, if we only give people the temporal consequences of sin we will never do them any eternal good. The gospel after all is not merely about escaping STDs, prison, dysfunctional homes, broken marriages, abusive relationship, sexual addictions, or loneliness; the gospel has everything to do with how the wrath of God will be diverted from the sinner so that he/she will not spend an eternity in Hell, where they will suffer unspeakable and unbearable conscious torment because of God's unrelenting wrath. Jesus said:

Matthew 5:29–30 [29] "If your right eye makes you stumble, tear it out and throw it from you; for it is better for you to lose one of the parts of your body, than for your whole body to be thrown into hell. [30] If your right hand makes you stumble, cut it off and throw it from you; for it is better for you to lose one of the parts of your body, than for your whole body to go into hell."

Matthew 8:12 [12] "but the sons of the kingdom will be cast out into the outer darkness; in that place there will be weeping and gnashing of teeth."

Matthew 18:8–9 [8] "If your hand or your foot causes you to stumble, cut it off and throw it from you; it is better for you to enter life crippled or lame, than to have two hands or two feet and be cast into the eternal fire. [9] If your eye causes you to stumble, pluck it out and throw it from you. It is better for you to enter life with one eye, than to have two eyes and be cast into the fiery hell."

Matthew 25:46 [46] "These will go away into eternal punishment, but the righteous into eternal life."

As intolerable as the doctrine of Hell may be, it cannot be so intolerable that we will not preach it or we have not preached the gospel faithfully. Hell answers the question of what sin deserves, Hell answers the question of what God thinks of sin and sinners who violate His perfect standard of righteousness and fall short of His glory, Hell answers the questions of where a person will go if they do not repent and believe in the gospel. Without preaching the wages of sin, we will only preach a therapeutic moralistic message that will not instill the fear of the Lord in anyone.

The dreadful condition of the sinner and the miserable end they face drove Puritan Joseph Alleine to preach much on the subject of the unconverted during his brief life on earth. Contemplating the reality of the sinner's plight, he says, "It is therefore of high necessity that I not only convince men that they are unconverted—but that I also endeavor to bring them to a sense of the fearful misery of this state." Alleine goes on to talk about the blindness of the unbeliever and his inability to see the misery he is in:

> "Could I bring paradise into view—or represent the kingdom of heaven to as much advantage as the tempter did the kingdoms of the world, and the glory thereof, to our Savior; or could I uncover the face of the deep and devouring gulf of Hell in all its terrors, and open the gates of the infernal furnace; alas, he has no eyes to see it! Could I paint the beauties of holiness, or the glory of the Gospel; or could I expose to view the more than diabolical deformity and ugliness of sin; he can no more judge of the loveliness and beauty of the one, and the filthiness and hatefulness of the other, than a blind man of colors. He is alienated from the life of God, through the ignorance that is in him because of the blindness of his heart (Eph 4:18). He neither knows nor can know—the things of God, because they are spiritually discerned (1 Cor. 2:14). His eyes cannot be savingly opened but by converting grace (Acts 26:18). He is a child of darkness, and walks in darkness. Yes, the light in him is darkness."[31]

I would quote a more contemporary voice, but the sad reality is that many today simply refuse to write on the subject of Hell at all, a cor-

---

[31]Joseph Alleine (1634-1668), *An Alarm to the Unconverted* (Lafayette: Sovereign Grace Publishers, 2002) p.54.

rection that should be made in today's Evangelical and even Reformed churches. It seems that we may have bought into the culture's caricature of the 'Hellfire and brimstone preacher' so that we do not ever want to be labeled as such. Jesus clearly would have been labeled such a preacher and who are we to suppose that we are greater than our Master?

The sinner is under the curse of the Law, partially implying that sinners cannot free themselves from this curse. The weight is too great, the standard is too high, the goal is too far out of reach; the sinner's only hope is to look to Christ as the merciful Savior to save him. Throughout the history of the church, and in particular, with the Reformers, there has always been an understanding that this is the crux of the issue when it comes to understanding God's grace and the nature of salvation. In his article, *The Reflections of a Puritan Theologian on Regeneration and Conversion*, Michael Haykin takes us beyond the more well known Reformation subject of justification to the deeper issue of the sinner's inability:

> "At the heart of the Reformation was one of the most fundamental questions of the Christian faith: How can I be saved from eternal damnation? The answer of all the leading Reformers was one and the same: only by God's free and sovereign grace. As J. I. Packer and O. Raymond Johnston have pointed out, it is wrong to suppose that the doctrine of Justification by faith alone, that storm center of the Reformation, was *the* crucial question in the minds of such theologians as Martin Luther, Ulrich Zwingli, Martin Bucer, and John Calvin. This doctrine was important to the Reformers because it helped to express and to safeguard their answer to another, more vital, question, namely, whether sinners are wholly helpless in their sin, and whether God is to be thought of as saving them by free, unconditional, invincible grace, not only justifying them for Christ's sake when they come to faith, but also raising them from the death of sin by His quickening Spirit in order to bring them to faith."[32]

[32]Michael A. G. Haykin, Reformation and Revival Journal, RAR 05:3 (Summer 1996), *The Reflections of a Puritan Theologian on Regeneration and Conversion*. As Haykin points out in the Journal, the Puritans were "equally insistent" on the misery of the sinner and their inability to save themselves so that salvation was always viewed as a gift of God grounded in "free grace alone".

It is the consistent testimony of Scripture and Church History that God saves sinners apart from anything good in us. It is neither some sort of power within ourselves, potential or prevenient grace presented to us, but only by the free and sovereign grace of God found in the cross-work of Christ alone.

"...having become a curse for us" (Gal 3.13).

Sin is only one aspect in theology which the cross completes. Like many other things, it is not until we understand the relationship of a subject to the cross that we truly understand the nature of that subject. Sin is no exception. Only as we see the penalty which Christ had to pay for sin will we truly appreciate the wickedness of sin and the misery of sinners. The recent systematic theology by J. van Genderen and W.H. Velema draws out the significance of pointing us to the cross for a fuller understanding of sin and the predicament the cross puts a sinner in:

> "It must be pointed out that *knowledge of sin does not only come about through the law.* In this regard Berkouwer appropriately quotes the words of Bavinck "that true repentance, real sorrow over sin and genuine return to God and his service definitely come about not only through the law but *also and even more so* through the gospel"... It is noteworthy that Bavinck here makes the comparisons (*comparativus*) of "not only, but also and even more so." What could Bavinck mean by this? To our mind he means that the gospel is also a source of knowledge of our misery. Why is this the case? It is because the gospel continues to confront us with the law; it is the good news that Christ has met the requirement of the law. The fulfillment of the requirement of the law comprises a twofold obedience, namely, to fulfill the commandments of God *and* to suffer the curse of the law. Precisely the cross of Christ reveals how serious sin is."[33]

The cross delivers the final bone crushing blow to the pride of the sinner. The reason is because the obedience and suffering which the Law demanded could never be accomplished by us. In this way, we are made to feel the full weight of the Law; not only because the Law says we are guilty for specific crimes e.g. 'do not lie, do not murder, do not steal' etc,

---

[33] J. van Generen, W.H. Velema, *Concise Reformed Dogmatics* (Phillipsburg: P&R, 2008) p.432.

but 'also and even more so' because the cross shows us that we are impotent to absolve ourselves of those crimes (cf. Ps. 49.7-12). All one can do is look to Christ in faith (Lk. 23.42-43).

In a very real and practical sense I can readily testify to the efficacy of the cross in making a person comprehend their guilt. I can remember my own conversion, an overnight Damascus road experience that brought me out of darkness into light. That event, which was so powerfully earth shattering, was truly an emotional time for me. But I remember feeling the shame of my sin and the condemnation I deserved, yet upon reflection, it was when I contemplated the cross that my understanding of sin and grace was greatly magnified. Though I could never have articulated it then, the cross explained the cost Christ had to pay for my guilt and sin. It also showed me the awful truth that I was powerless to deliver myself from my sins. This seems to be what Paul was thinking when he said, "*I have been crucified with Christ; and it is no longer I who live, but Christ lives in me; and the life which I now live in the flesh I live by faith in the Son of God, who loved me and gave Himself up for me. "I do not nullify the grace of God, for if righteousness comes through the Law, then Christ died needlessly." (Gal. 2.20-21).

Therefore, it is through the cross that those who were under the curse of the Law could be redeemed from the curse of the Law *because* Christ Himself was cursed for us i.e. crucified.[34] Christ became our curse bearer. He shows us what the wages of sin demand, namely God's dreadful curse. Either man will bear his/her own curse, or Christ will take the curse for them. Every attempt to justify ourselves will only result in greater guilt since we are unable to perform *all* that the Law demands:

Galatians 3:10–13 [10] "For as many as are of the works of the Law are under a curse; for it is written, "Cursed is everyone who does not abide by all things written in the book of the law, to perform them." [11] Now that no one is justified by the Law before God is evident; for, "The righteous man shall live by faith." [12] However, the Law is not of faith; on the contrary, "He who practices them shall live by them." [13] Christ redeemed us from the curse of the Law, having become a curse for us—for it is written, "Cursed is everyone who hangs on a tree."

---

[34]See below: chapter four.

The ominous truth of sin and sinners is that they stand under a *curse* (καταρα), God's divine imprecation for every person who has broken God's Laws and tramples the blood of His Son underfoot in unbelief. And furthermore, as the sinner attempts self-justification the more the weight of the Law will bear down upon him. Because righteousness could only be merited through perfect obedience to the Law, "no one is justified by the Law before God" (Gal. 3.11a: cf. Rom. 4.1-8). Making men sensible to their sin is making them aware that they are under a divine curse, incurred by breaking a divine and holy Law, understood by the price Christ had to pay on the cross. When we speak of God's laws, these are not simply the Laws of pious prophets or religious devotees; it is the Law which reflects the very nature and righteousness of God Himself. Under this curse, man is ordained to suffer the penalty of the curse by God's own appointment and choice. This is why the curse is so unbearable; God stands as executioner of the curse incurred by our sin. The curse does not simply act on its own behalf, the consequences are rather enforced by God Himself. Modern Puritan, commentator, and Biblical expositor John Brown explains:

> " 'To be made a curse' " is a strong expression for become accursed; or, in other words, being subjected, by the Divine appointment, to that suffering, the infliction of which sin had rendered necessary for the honour of the Divine character and government,—that suffering which is the manifestation of the Divine displeasure at sin."[35]

In Galatians 3.10 Paul is quoting from Deuteronomy 27.26, "Cursed is he who does not confirm the words of this law by doing them…". If we look at some of the features of the context of Deuteronomy 27&28, we find that central to everything being spoken there was this idea of blessing and cursing. The blessings and the curses are pretty straight forward: you will be blessed for obedience and cursed for disobedience (e.g. 'Cursed is he…' Deut. 27.26; 28.15f, and, 'All these blessings will come upon you… if…' Deut. 28.2). Those were the stipulations of the covenant God made with Israel. It was a tall order however, the standard of the Law demands perfect obedience, an obedience that no one was ever capable of keeping in totality, perfectly, and exhaustively (Deut. 28.1).

---

[35]John Brown, *Galatians, Geneva Series of Commentaries* (Carlisle: Banner of Truth, 2001) p.131

While Israel often experienced curses which pertained to land, wars, captivity, and fertility, the ultimate punishment for God's curse is nothing less than eternal destruction. After asserting that under sin and under the curse of Galatians, there we are 'corrupt and condemned' John Piper specifies, "The consequence of this curse and wrath is eternal misery apart from the glory of God".[36] This is why Paul calls the Law under the Mosaic Covenant 'the ministry of condemnation' (2 Cor. 3.7). Because man is sinful, we are in need of a new heart which delights in doing God's will without which the Law could only produce death (Rom. 7. 7-12 cf. 1 Jn. 5.3). That Christ died under God's curse is tremendously good news because in this act of suffering and death, Christ saves us and simultaneously glorifies God. Thus, the curse implies justice, substitution, imputation, sacrifice, and atonement, which secures both the justification of God's people and the honor of God's justice. Again Brown demonstrates the rigorous theological thought progression of this passage:

> "The language of the text, and of the many other texts in which Christ's sufferings and death are presented as undergone in the room [i.e. *in place*] of his people, by no means necessarily implies that Christ experienced precisely the same kind and degree of suffering that they must have done had he not interfered—a reflecting mind will soon perceive that this is a statement which involves in it many difficulties—but it does teach us, that the sufferings which Christ endured were sufferings on account of the sins of his people; and sufferings which satisfied the law, or in other words, rendered it right, safe, and honourable in God to pardon sin, and save those in whose room they were sustained— those who, in the appointed way, were united to him who sustained them."[37]

To preach Christ crucified is to tell sinners that they are under a curse and in order to understand sin for what it is they must understand why Christ was cursed and who He was cursed for. Paul says, "Christ redeemed us from the curse of the Law, having become a curse for us" (Gal. 3.13a). Christ was cursed *for us* (ὑπὲρ ἡμῶν) meaning 'on our behalf' or

[36]John Piper, *When I Don't Desire God, How to Fight for Joy* (Wheaton: Crossway Books, 2004) p.72.

[37]John Brown, *Galatians*; p.132. (brackets mine).

as Brown states, "on account of the sins of his people" because it was the only way to remove the curse from us.

However, Christ was not cursed because He could not or did not fulfill every stipulation of the Law; He most certainly did (Jn. 8.29). It was precisely Christ's perfect obedience to the Law which qualified Jesus to redeem His people from beneath the curse (Phil. 2.6-11; Heb. 5.8-9). Timothy George commenting on what he called the "counter-curse"[38] says:

> "Apart from Jesus' perfect obedience of the law, what happened at Calvary would have had no more redemptive significance than the brutal crucifixion of thousands of other young Jews before, during, and after the earthly life of Christ."[39]

His curse did not consist in His disobedience but in ours. Though He was innocent of all charges, though He had met all of the just requirements of the Law, yet, He laid down His life *voluntarily* (Jn. 10.15; Mt. 20.28; Mk. 10.45). God cursed Christ not because He disobeyed, but because He willfully took upon Himself the sin and disobedience of the world (2 Cor. 5.21). John the Baptist said, "Behold, the Lamb of God who takes away the sin of the world! " (John 1.29). It was precisely because of this willful act of substitution that God's curse was placed on Jesus; not for disobeying but for *hanging on a tree* in our place (Gal. 3.13b; Gal. 2.20). In the latter part of Galatians 3.13, Paul is pulling from another Old Testament quotation when referring to Christ's curse, "his corpse shall not hang all night on the tree, but you shall surely bury him on the same day (for he who is hanged is accursed of God)" (Dt. 21.23). On the suffering of Christ and its meaning for the believer after the fact, Leon Morris has observed the great import of the cross for Christian theology on the subject of suffering. Morris points out that the believer's own calling to suffer is predicated upon the pattern which our 'Master' Himself set forth in His cross-work:

> "The truth is that, for the Christian, suffering has been trans-formed by the fact that his Master came to suffer. Both our Gospels have a good deal to say about the sufferings of Christ, and these sufferings have saving power. These sufferings cannot be

---

[38]Timothy George, vol. 30, *Galatians, The New American Commentary* (Nashville: Broadman & Holman Publishers, 2001) p.233. 39

[39]Ibid, p.236.

regarded as no more than the outcome of the machinations of wicked men. They are that. But they are also, and more importantly, the means whereby God brings blessing to mankind. The pathway to salvation lies through sufferings, the sufferings of the Son of God Himself."[40]

There can be no doubt then, that Christ's suffering and death had many implications. For example our sanctification. Other aspects of His suffering pertain to an imitation of Him throughout our personal and progressive sanctification. Christ crucified instructs us in many ways. Continuing the curse-bearing motif however of this death, it was common practice in OT times that criminals under various capital offenses were often stoned to death and then hung publicly to shamefully display that this person was indeed cursed by God. It spoke of God's rejection, it spoke of being guilty of sin and trespass, it spoke of humiliation and often times would be done to add insult to injury, in essence saying, "This person has been justly executed." Thus Peter charges the Jews for the murder of Jesus who they *put to death* as a criminal (Acts 2.23).

As unjust as the death of Christ was by the hands of 'godless men', the gospel is good news nonetheless. This text in Galatians brings the matter into greater focus as to why, and who the news is for; not simply sinners, but sinners who are not only under a curse, but have no power to deliver themselves from this curse. Leon Morris reminds us of the glorious liberty Christ secures *for* us by taking sin's curse *from* us:

> "The curse means a death sentence and sinners are ransomed from this by the death of Jesus. Paul does not let his readers escape from the truth that sin is serious, for it brings God's curse on the sinner. But he insists just as firmly on the truth that those who put their trust in Christ have nothing to fear. They are redeemed, brought out of the effect of the curse that rested on them, and brought into the glorious liberty of the people of God."[41]

While we deserved to be cursed for our disobedience, Christ took our sin upon Himself and in our place. He was counted as a virtual criminal for the sake of real criminals (Is. 53. 12). This is an act of substitution,

---

[40]Leon L. Morris, *The Cross in the New Testament* (Grand Rapids: Eerdmans, 1999) p.26.

[41]Leon Morris, *Galatians Paul's Character of Christian Freedom* (Downers Grove: IVP, 1996) p.106-107.

this is the process of imputation,[42] and this, stepping in to the place of sinners, is what Peter calls, "the just for the unjust that He might bring us to God" (1 Pet. 3.18). In this way Jesus was "made... to be sin" ($\dot{\alpha}\mu\alpha\rho\tau\acute{\iota}$ $\alpha\nu$ $\dot{\epsilon}\pi o\acute{\iota}\eta\sigma\epsilon\nu$):

> **2 Corinthians 5:21** [21] "He made Him who knew no sin to be sin on our behalf, so that we might become the righteousness of God in Him."

Apart from faith in the Christ who was cursed for us, we remain under the curse, forced to endure the curse on our own and if we will endure our own curse, we will endure our own death and Hell. To preach Christ crucified is thus to present to sinners the wonder of imputation. where everything we lost in Adam and sin. we gain in Christ by faith. It was these marvelous truths from Galatians which caused Luther exult in Christ' cross-work:

> "We are ignorant of God, enemies of God, dead in sin, and cursed. What can we deserve? There is no way we can avoid the curse except to believe and with assured confidence say, " 'You, Christ, are my sin and my curse; or rather, I am your sin, your curse, your death, your wrath of God, your hell. Conversely, you are my righteousness, my blessing, my life, my grace of God, and my heaven.' "[43]

As we have seen, when it pertains to making men sensible of their misery, the phrase "through the cross" is not superfluous but necessary. It is not until we bring sinners not merely before the bar of God's Law, as absolutely necessary as this is, but beneath the shadow of the cross that people will truly grasp the weight of their sin, the misery of the curse, and the redemption which Christ provides through the infinite price He paid on the cross. John Murray draws attention to the great "costliness" of that redemption purchased on the cross:

> "The cross of Christ is the supreme demonstration of the love of God (Rom. 5:8; 1 Jn. 4.10). The supreme character of the demonstration resides in the extreme *costliness* of the sacrifice

---

[42] More will be said on imputation, substitution, and justification in chapters three and four.
[43] Martin Luther, *Galatians, The Crossway Classic Commentaries*, Ed. Alister McGrath, J.I. Packer (Wheaton: Crossway Books, 1998) p.157.

rendered… The costliness of the sacrifice assures us of the greatness of the love and guarantees the bestowal of all other free gifts…. Without it we are bereft of the elements necessary to make intelligible to us the meaning of Calvary and the marvel of its supreme love to us men."[44]

Paul told the Romans much the same thing, namely that Jesus was lovingly and by the forbearance of God, placated as the crucified Messiah who has come at the perfect time to redeem His people (Gal. 4.4). In this way, Christ bore the wrath of God on the cross or *in His blood* which is Pauline *code* for Jesus' cross-work (Rom. 3.25). Paul insists the cross was to demonstrate the righteousness of God. In other words, when we look to the cross and point others to the cross-work of Christ, we see something of the righteousness of God in it. The righteousness of God's own nature and character, the righteousness of His Son, the righteousness God demands, and the righteousness He accepts; all marvelously and mercifully placated for us at the cross.

Therefore, in order to faithfully preach Christ we must never fall short of preaching how the cross makes sinners sensible of their misery. The cross is not something we tack on at the end of our gospel presentation once all the real work has been done; the cross is the glorious epicenter of the gospel. This is why Paul could so fearlessly remind the Corinthians of his Christocentric gospel message, "For I determined to know nothing among you except Jesus Christ, and Him crucified" (1 Cor. 2.2). We do not disjoin the Law from the cross, we show *through* the cross how burdensome the Law really is and just how guilty man is if he forsakes such a great salvation. It is at the cross where sin is fully exposed for what it is, what it requires, and how God has dealt with it through the blood of His own Son. Through the cross, people can be shown both the intolerance of God with regards to sin, and the patience of God with regards to sinners. At the cross the words of the Psalmist are quintessentially fulfilled:

"Mercy and truth have met together,
Righteousness and peace have kissed each other."

— Psalm 85:10

---

[44]John Murray, *Redemption Accomplished and Applied* (Grand Rapids: Eerdmans, 1955) p.17. (*emphasis mine*).

3

CRUCIFIED FOR OUR PEACE, PREACHING THE GOODNESS OF GOD IN JUSTIFYING THE UNGODLY

Quite possibly one of the reasons why our evangelism suffers today in the evangelical church is due to the diminishing of the doctrine of justification. In chapter one, I have made the case for election being brought back into the theological arsenal of the believer, for evangelism and the Christian faith. In chapter two, the cross was shown to be, not simply peripheral with regards to making men aware of their sin, but central. In essence, we are moving right along in the doctrine of salvation.

Election deals with man's eternity, sin deals with man's depravity, and now we must understand how God, not only justifies the ungodly, but how He does it in a way which renders Him just in doing so. One frequent objection I have heard leveled against the Christian worldview has to do with this question of Justification. Although perhaps unbelievers will not ask, "How does God remain just in justifying the ungodly?" They may say it In these ways:

"How can God just forgive rotten people? That's ridiculous!"

"So you mean to tell me that all I have to do is except Jesus into my heart?"

"I can live like the devil and ask for forgiveness before I die and everything will be ok, how is that fair?"

These criticisms reveal, not only, fundamental misunderstandings regarding the Christian position, but the great need for our evangelists to be equipped with a proper view of Justification; a position that will adequately and biblically answer all of the 'how is that possible' and 'that sounds ridiculous' or 'that is not fair' questions. To be sure, Scripture teaches rather emphatically that man in his fallen condition cannot properly discern spiritual things:

1 Corinthians 2:14 [14] "But a natural man does not accept the things of the Spirit of God, for they are foolishness to him; and he cannot understand them, because they are spiritually appraised."

This is because as Paul has already said, God is going to make the wise of this world foolish (1 Cor. 1.19, 20), His message cannot be understood through the wisdom of this world (1.18, 21), and His wisdom must be *revealed* (2.6-10). Yet the cross and a crucified Savior must still be preached (1 Cor. 2.2). Regardless of man's spiritual condition, there is no shortage of 'cross-talk' in Scripture. As Leon Morris puts it, "the cross dominates the New Testament".[45]

One major incentive for a cross-centered focus with regards to the doctrine of Justification and how that relates to sinners is, of course, the fact that the cross is where all of salvation is bound up. This is what the Corinthians once considered *foolishness* (μωρία). The reality is that people, unbelievers in particular, but believers as well may be confused about Justification. More precisely, Christian evangelism, and those engaged in it, must possess a robust and biblically informed theology of Justification in order to effectively communicate how a person comes into a right relationship with God.[46] Chapter two was about the sinner's lack of merit before God, in a negative sense it is his 'demerit'. This chapter deals positively with the sinner's righteousness and precisely how his demerit can be overcome so that he can posses a positive righteousness so as to be accepted by God apart from human merit altogether. The doctrine of Justification is all about how we can be accepted by a righteous God.

---

[45]Leon Morris, *The Cross in the New Testament*, p.365.

[46]A small bibliography is in order at this point for those who want to read more in depth volumes on the subject: John Murray, *Redemption Accomplished and Applied* (1955). James Buchanan, *The Doctrine of Justification* (based on the Cunningham Lectures of 1866). James White, *The God Who Justifies* (2001). J.V. Fesko, *Justification, Understanding the Classic Reformed Doctrine* (2008). Also see, Systematics: Wayne Grudem, *Systematic Theology* (1994). Robert L. Reymond, *A New Systematic Theology of the Christian Faith* (1998). However much I may disagree with all of these authors at various points, all are worth reading and studying carefully.

Justification is about Righteousness

Through the years, I have had several evangelistic encounters with Muslims of various backgrounds. Although like all evangelistic encounters each exchange with Muslims has been wide and varied, still, a common note always seems to leave the same impression; they have no peace with God. Whether we are speaking with Muslims or not, all sinners have this in common, that they have no peace with God being outside of Jesus Christ. Sticking with the Muslim for a moment, the truth of matter is; when Muslims pray five times a day they have no peace with God, when Muslims fast on Ramadan they have no peace with God, when Muslims travel to Mecca on pilgrimage they have no peace with God, and when they recite the words of the Quran, they are hopelessly at enmity with God. Why? They lack the righteousness God demands.

Unfortunately, many gospel presentations present false dilemmas to people through *Moralism*—arguing that people need to simply behave better, *Postmodernism*—arguing that people simply need to 'try Jesus' as one of many options on the menu of world religions, or *Psychology*—arguing that if people come to Christ they can be delivered from all forms of mental and dysfunctional disorders both in family and culture. To be sure, Christ does transform (2 Cor. 5.17). He causes us to be holy and live righteously in this present evil age (Tit. 2.12), Christ also heals deep wounds of all marital, familial, or social types (Tit. 3.3); yet Christ, as is often pointed out, does not simply save us from our dysfunctional families, but from the wrath of an infinitely holy and righteous God. This is why if we are going to faithfully preach Christ, the only dilemma worth focusing on is that dilemma presented to us in the gospel. That means that Muslims, Atheists, Agnostics, and the dear old woman in the convalescent home have no peace with God and that neither their religiosity, intellectualism, nor moralistic therapy will provide them the peace they need. I realize it sounds desperate, it is. The only thing that can produce this peace is righteousness, specifically the righteousness that God demands and the righteousness that Christ possesses.

Even more specifically however, regarding the righteousness which God demands, we are speaking of the righteousness of Christ. Only this righteousness will do. The doctrine of justification forces us outside of ourselves and toward an alien foreign righteousness that must be appropriated by faith. Paul set it forth this way:

Philippians 3:7–9 [7] "But whatever things were gain to me, those things I have counted as loss for the sake of Christ. [8] More than that, I count all things to be loss in view of the surpassing value of knowing Christ Jesus my Lord, for whom I have suffered the loss of all things, and count them but rubbish so that I may gain Christ, [9] and may be found in Him, not having a righteousness of my own derived from the Law, but that which is through faith in Christ, the righteousness which comes from God on the basis of faith…"

The context is polemical, Paul begins this chapter with a dire triple warning to the believers in Philippi, "beware of the dogs, beware of the evil workers, beware of the false circumcision"[47] (Phil. 3.2). Paul who has the unique qualifications of boasting in the accomplishments of the flesh refuses to do so (cf. Phil. 3.3-6). Instead, Paul argues for the futility of trying to derive your righteousness from self-originated works based on Law observance. In fact, he considers self-originated righteousness as 'rubbish' ($\sigma\kappa\acute{\upsilon}\beta\alpha\lambda o\nu$). Only upon conversion can the sinner see his own righteousness in this light (Is. 57.12; 64.6).

But a conversion conceived to be originating due to forces outside of ourselves is quite unintelligible in our world. Our generation, possibly more than ever, is locked inside of itself seeing no need for an external deliverance or a divine 'Deliverer' for that matter. David Wells speaks to precisely this issue, perhaps better than anyone else today; he points to the rise of individual subjectivism, the human obsession with self and what he calls 'modern individuality' and 'our own hidden resources'. Wells is quoted at length here:

> "The subjective obsession that also confronts us in religious dress (as is often the case in evangelicalism) sometimes appears in dress that is quite irreligious. Whatever the garb, however it exhibits the same underlying mentality, the same habits of man, the same assumption that reality can be accessed only through the self (and by intuition rather than by thought), the same belief that

---

[47] The Greek text is much more explicit and brutal here, "the false circumcision" (NASB) is literally 'the mutilation' ($\kappa\alpha\tau\alpha\tau o\mu\acute{\eta}$) thus, (ESV, NIV, NET). Under Jewish Law, mutilation was a violation of the Levitical code (e.g. (Lev. 19.28; 21.5; Dt. 14.1; Is. 15.2; Hos. 7.14). This then would be almost a satirical way of describing the Judaizers who were influencing the Philippians towards circumcision.

we can attain virtually unlimited personal progress if only we can tap into our own hidden resources. This fascination with the self, made bright with hope by the belief in progress, has proved to be a gold mine for publishers. In the overall religious book market today, 31 percent of all books sold fall into the inspiration and motivational category, and further 15 percent work these same themes from a New Age angel."[48]

As we will see from the words of Wells below, Philosophy has joined with Modernity to produce slaves of self on a very complex and formidable level. Making matters worse is the reality that the world is quite skilled in exploiting man's fascination with autonomy in general. Being saved is a weakness, 'saviors' are superstitions, and guilt through sin and the divine law is old fashioned—'ideologies' which are quite incompatible with the 'progress' of 21st century man. For Wells, this 'modern individualism' is nothing short of a reordering of reality:

"There is, of course, a certain affinity between the Enlightenment vision of the human being at the center of reality, fashioning the world in better and more pleasing way, and this new modern person who looks for reality only in the self. The modern, self-absorbed individualist is in continuity with the Enlightenment ideal but, in most cases, is not the direct product of the Enlightenment. This person is also the product of the modernization that has been brought about by market economies, technology, urbanization, bureaucracies, and mass communication. The collective effect of these products of modernization—modernity—has coalesced with Enlightenment ideals to produce the new individualist: the Enlightenment posits ultimate authority in the self, and modernity severs the self from any meaningful connections outside itself. Thus, the inward and outward environment become as one; they depend on and reinforce each other. This confluence of thought and social environment has produced great turbulence and disorder in the modern psyche. It has reshaped the modern understanding of who people are, how they gain access to reality, and how they should govern their behavior."[49]

---

[48]David F. Wells, *No Place for Truth Or Whatever Happened to Evangelical Theology* (Grand Rapids: Eerdmans, 1993) pp.142-143.

[49]Ibid, p.143.

Unlike the subjectivists of every age, Paul understood that the ground of our righteousness was outside of self altogether; outside of us and *in Christ* (ἐν Χριστῷ). There could be no other basis from which we could derive our righteousness except from what Christ Himself did on the cross. This is because, as Paul has stated, faith is how we obtain "the righteousness which comes from God" (Phil. 3.9b). Charles Hodge highlights this very thing:

> "Every believer relies for his acceptance with God, not on himself but on Christ, not on what he is or has done, but on what Christ is and has done for him. By the righteousness of Christ is meant all He became, did, and suffered to satisfy the demand of divine justice and to merit for His people forgiveness of sin and the gift of eternal life… The righteousness of Christ on the ground of which the believer is justified is the righteousness of God."[50]

In a world where people are meticulous, even experts in self-justification, the call to abandon self, as the source of what qualifies as acceptable to God, is not an easy task. Biblically speaking, the doctrine of Justification assumes that man is guilty, desperate, and incapable of producing the righteousness God demands. *God wants His own righteousness in sinners.* In order to accomplish this however, it must be earned. Ironically, there is a sense in which one could say, salvation is 'by works' (i.e. Christ's works). Scripture often defines the meritorious righteousness of Christ as obedience:

Philippians 2:5–11 [5] "Have this attitude in yourselves which was also in Christ Jesus, [6] who, although He existed in the form of God, did not regard equality with God a thing to be grasped, [7] but emptied Himself, taking the form of a bond-servant, and being made in the likeness of men. [8] Being found in appearance as a man, He humbled Himself by becoming obedient to the point of death, even death on a cross. [9] For this reason also, God highly exalted Him, and bestowed on Him the name which is above every name, [10] so that at the name of Jesus every knee will bow, of those who are in heaven and on earth and under the earth, [11] and that every tongue will confess that Jesus Christ is Lord, to the glory of God the Father."

[50]Charles Hodge, *Systematic Theology*, Abridged Edition edited by Edward N. Gross (Grand Rapids: Baker Book House, 1988) p.459.

Hebrews 5:8–9 [8] "Although He was a Son, He learned obedience from the things which He suffered. [9] And having been made perfect, He became to all those who obey Him the source of eternal salvation."

Romans 5:18–19 [18] "So then as through one transgression there resulted condemnation to all men, even so through one act of righteousness there resulted justification of life to all men. [19] For as through the one man's disobedience the many were made sinners, even so through the obedience of the One the many will be made righteous."

Jesus Himself was cognizant of the fact that His purpose was to glorify the Father through His life of perfect obedience, "For I have come down from heaven, not to do My own will, but the will of Him who sent Me" (Jn. 6.38). He never failed at this. He was always and perfectly obedient to the divine will of the Father, "… I always do the things that are pleasing to Him" (Jn. 8.29b). This was, of course, because the will of the Son and the will of the Father were inseparably bound in purpose and design, "Truly, truly, I say to you, the Son can do nothing of Himself, unless it is something He sees the Father doing; for whatever the Father does, these things the Son also does in like manner" (Jn. 5.19). Jesus was never out of sync with God's will because He Himself was as much God as His Father. Jesus always did what the Father gave Him to do because the Father's will for Christ was something both Father and Son had agreed on from eternity. Thus, Christ's obedience was bound to the plan of redemption conceived in eternity and crystallized in time. This is the work Jesus set out to do and accomplished and it is this work which is acceptable to God and is imputed to the believer (Jn. 17.1-4).

But sinners are always out of sync with God's will, before conversion they do not possess the capacity to please God (Rom. 8.7). No matter how hard they may try, no matter how much they may claim to love God, to appreciate or respect Him, if they have not been given a new heart to delight in God's will, they will never live according to God's will thus, they will remain at enmity with God. This is what John Murray meant when he said, "we are all wrong with him":

"And we all are all wrong with him because we all have sinned and come short of the glory of God. Far too frequently we fail to entertain the gravity of this fact. Hence the reality of our sin and the reality of the wrath of God upon us for our sin do not come into our reckoning. This is the reason why the grand article of justification does not ring the bells in the innermost depths of our spirit. And this is the reason why the gospel of justification is to such an extent a meaningless sound in the world and in the church of the twentieth century. We are not imbued with the profound sense of the reality of God, of his majesty and holiness. And sin, if reckoned with at all, is little more than a misfortune or maladjustment."[51]

When we misunderstand 'the grand article of justification' in our gospel presentation we fail to tell people the truth about themselves and God. We do not show man his sin and the fact that he is 'all wrong' with God. We fail in declaring the very 'majesty and holiness' of God of which Murray speaks. Too often we preach cheap grace, we teach therapy not theology, and we preach self-esteem, moralism, or emotionalism and not Christ crucified. In surrendering such parameters of the gospel we will seek for a softer more palatable message—one which we might be tempted to think man can more readily identify with. This may be true, but we strip the gospel of its bare essentials and power (cf. 1 Cor. 2.5); that man is infinitely sinful, that the Law is infinitely holy, that God is infinitely gracious, and that Christ's cross-work is infinitely precious for justifying sinners. This is why we must convince people of their sin and misery as outlined in chapter two. Who better than Jonathan Edwards to remind us this:

> "They must be sensible that they are the children of wrath; that the law is against them, and that they are exposed to the curse of it: that the wrath of God abideth on them; and that he is angry with them every day while they are under the guilt of sin."[52]

Justification is about Grace

The righteousness of God is rooted in God's grace. If it does not come to us as a result of works, that is, our works, it must be bestowed upon us as a result of grace. There also is a lot of confusion about the role of faith and justification. Is our faith what justifies us? Is our faith a work?

---

[51]John Murray, *Redemption Accomplished and Applied*, p.117

[52]Jonathan Edwards, *Jonathan Edwards on Knowing Christ* (Carlisle: Banner of Truth, 1997) p.267.

Scripture never refers to faith being the basis of our justification—an important distinction to make if the gospel of God's grace is to be maintained. The power is not so much in the power of *faith* but in the power of faiths' *object*. It has more to do with what we place our faith in than that we have faith. With so much contemporary dialogue today in media, entertainment, and other public platforms (not to mention some churches); faith is made out to be more important than God. Politicians, athletes, actors and actresses, often tout the power of faith. One example on this was *The New York Times* 2004 article on the faith of President George W. Bush entitled, *Faith, Certainty and the Presidency of George W. Bush*, where journalist Ron Suskind focused on what he referred to as the 'efficacy' of the president's faith. Suskind spoke of faith as if it were a power in and of itself. Faith intervened in Bush's alcoholism, faith healed his marriage, faith gave him wisdom in the oval office, and faith is even spoken about as if it were salvation itself—something people of all religions are capable of and, as is implied, should even view as effective regardless of 'denominational' background or religion. Faith is given absolute prominence. During Bush's "darkest hour" when the decision came to deploy troops to Afghanistan following the attacks of September 11th, Suskind writes of the prominence of faith in the life of President Bush and all Americans who exercised their faith by supporting the President through prayer:

> "Within a few days of the attacks, Bush decided on the invasion of Afghanistan and was barking orders. His speech to the joint session of Congress on Sept. 20 will most likely be the greatest of his presidency. He prayed for God's help. And many Americans, of all faiths, prayed with him—or for him. It was simple and nondenominational: a prayer that he'd be up to this moment, so that he—and, by extension, we as a country—would triumph in that dark hour. This is where the faith-based presidency truly takes shape. Faith, which for months had been coloring the decision-making process and a host of political tactics—think of his address to the nation on stem-cell research—now began to guide events. It was the most natural ascension: George W. Bush turning to *faith* in his darkest moment and discovering a wellspring of power and confidence."[53]

[53]By Ron Suskind, Published: October 17, 2004: http://www.nytimes.com/2004/10/17/magazine/17BUSH.html?_r=1. (Italics mine).

Scripture makes a careful distinction between the role of faith and the role of faith's object. Had president Bush, or any politician for that matter, given God or more precisely what God did through Jesus Christ the preeminence over faith itself, it would have hardly qualified as being politically correct. The object of justifying faith is Christ and His righteousness. Faith does not have faith in faith. Faith is the hand which receives the gift of God's righteousness resulting in the justification of the ungodly. Faith is the vehicle which carries Christ's righteousness to our account. Faith is the agent, grace is the anchor:

> **Romans 4:16** [16] "For this reason it is by faith, in order that it may be in accordance with grace, so that the promise will be guaranteed to all the descendants, not only to those who are of the Law, but also to those who are of the faith of Abraham, who is the father of us all..."

Faith is not a work, it is a gift, "to you it has been granted for Christ's sake, not only to believe in Him, but also to suffer for His sake," (Phil. 1.29). This is why faith cannot be counted as a work which arises out of man's own personal volitional activity. As Leon Morris has clearly stated, "The emphasis in Paul's writings is always on what God has done for man's salvation, not on any human effort whatever."[54] Had God not granted him faith, man would have never possessed it in the first place. Had faith been a work, then our justification would be owed to us like an employee's wages. Therefore, we should never present the gospel in such a way that communicates the idea that faith can merit salvation, it cannot. Here again Paul eliminates the possibility of being justified on the basis of faith as a work:

> **Romans 4:4–5** [4] "Now to the one who works, his wage is not credited as a favor, but as what is due. [5] But to the one who does not work, but believes in Him who justifies the ungodly, his faith is credited as righteousness, Paul is seeking to put righteousness far out of the realm of human merit."

Abraham was not justified because of any works. His faith is therefore not looked upon as a work (properly defined), but as a precondition for receiving God's righteousness—a precondition worked into us and

---

[54]Morris, *The Cross in the New Testament*, p.260.

granted to us by God's sovereign grace (2 Tim. 2.25 cf. Jn. 10.26). The Puritans were quite zealous to keep a proper distinction between faith and righteousness. They saw faith and justification in a proper relationship. In a famous chapter entitled, *Not Faith but Christ*, Scottish Puritan Horatius Bonar (1808-1889), emphatically dismissed our faith as the basis of our justification:

> "...*faith* is not our righteousness... Faith does not justify as a work, or as a moral act, or a piece of goodness nor as a gift of the Spirit, but simply because it is the bond between us and the Substitute— a very slender bond in one sense, but strong as iron in another. The work of Christ *for* us is the object of faith. The Spirit's work *in us* is that which produces this faith: it is out of the former, not the latter, that our peace and justification come... Faith is not our physician... Faith is not our savior... Faith is not perfection... Faith is not satisfaction to God... Faith is not Christ nor the cross of Christ... Faith is rest not toil... Christ is to be the burden of our preaching and the substance of our belief from first to last."[55]

Bonar states with great eloquence what others have argued with great exegetical rigor, namely that the NT nowhere makes faith the final cause of our justification as if the mere act of faith was righteous and meritorious—it is not. This has been proven in a number of ways. For example, any theology of faith and justification which tends towards making faith earn our justification runs contrary to Paul's argument against any human merit everywhere in his writings. Grammatically the issue is even clearer. Robert Reymond explains:

> "Never is our faith-act, however, represented in the New Testament as the ground or the cause of our righteousness. If this were so, faith would become a meritorious work, an idea everywhere opposed by the Apostle Paul who pits faith in Christ over against every human work. We are said to be justified "by faith" (the

[55]Horatius Bonar (1808-1889), *The Everlasting Righteousness, How Shall Man be Just with God?*: cited in *God's Gospel of Grace, The Doctrine of Salvation from the Pages of the Free Grace Broadcaster*. Chapel Library 2010; pp. 140-146. Also published as, *The Everlasting Righteousness* by Banner of Truth 1993. Also at this point see, *The Westminster Larger Catechism*, Q 73 which states that *faith* is the 'instrument through which we receive and apply Christ and *his* righteousness'.

simple dative—Rom. 3:28, 5:2), "by faith" (ἐκ, ek, with the genitive—Rom. 1:17; 3:30; 4:16 (twice), 5:1; 9:30; 10:6; Gal. 2:16; 3:8, 11, 24; Heb. 10:38), "through faith" (διά, dia, with the genitive—Rom. 3:22, 25, 30; Gal. 2:16; Phil. 3:9), "upon faith" (ἐπί, epi, with the genitive—Phil. 3:9), and "according to faith" (κατά, kata, with the accusative—Heb. 11:7). But never are we said to be justified "because of faith" or "on account of faith" (διά, dia, with the accusative). In other words, the psychic act of faith is not the righteousness of justification. That distinction the Scriptures reserve for Christ's God–righteousness alone. Faith in Christ is simply the regenerated sinner's saving response to God's effectual summons, by means of which the righteousness of Christ—the sole ground of justification—is imputed to him."[56]

This only magnifies the grace of God and shows that man in no way can save himself or even help God to save him. The authors of Scripture were very careful to describe the relationship between faith and justification in constructs which make clear that faith is not the basis of our righteousness, Christ is, and that faith is not the source of our justification, grace is. Joel Beeke points out the marvelous specificity of Scripture at this point when he says, "… such is the precision of the Spirit's overseeing of the New Testament Scriptures that nowhere does a writer slip into using this prepositional phrase (i.e. διά dia with the accusative). On every occasion, faith is presented as the *means* of justification."[57]

With faith in its proper relationship to God's righteousness we can agree with Paul that God has justified us freely "by His grace" (Rom. 3.24) apart from any "deeds which we have done" even "in righteousness"[58] (Tit. 3.5) God justifies 'by faith' in order that it might accord with

---

[56]Robert L. Reymond, *A New Systematic Theology of the Christian Faith*. p745.

[57]Joel R. Beeke, *Puritan Reformed Spirituality* (Grand Rapids: Reformation Heritage Books, 2004) p.379. [bracketed words are mine]

[58]The prepositional phrase is important in this text, οὐκ ἐξ ἔργων τῶν ἐν δικαιοσύνῃ ἃ ἐποιήσαμεν ἡμεῖς. The prepositional phrase, ἐν δικαιοσύνῃ "in righteousness", is functioning adverbially here to signify the religious quality of the "deeds" in focus. Even our religious deeds before and after salvation are not the basis of God justifying grace in saving us. Paul focuses on God's "mercy" (ἔλεος) as the true basis of salvation expanded upon here by the phrases, "the washing of regeneration" (λουτροῦ παλιγγενεσίας) and "renewing by the Holy Spirit" (καὶ ἀνακαινώσεως πνεύματος ἁγίυ).

"grace" (Rom. 4.16). Righteousness is about grace. A person cannot lay claim to God's righteousness because of baptism (as is often the case); whether church attendance, tithing, Scripture memorization, missionary activity, or mercy ministry—none of these can lay claim to the righteousness which is by grace through faith.

Ironically, it is this gospel of *free grace* which people disdain. Returning to our Muslim friends for a moment; Muslim men and women have no doctrine of atonement which satisfies God's justice like the gospel of Jesus Christ. Muslims will tell you they must take care of their sins on their own, again, by observing prayers, pilgrimages, and other religious particularities and superstitions—they see no need for the cross-work of Christ. In these ways they destroy the gospel of free grace and sink hopelessly into the abyss of legalism or what Paul refers to as "the weak and worthless elementary" principles of man (Gal. 4.9 cf. 4.3; Col. 2.8, 20). The issue is that man sees himself as self-determining and if they cannot work for salvation they will not receive it either. This is why part of God's grace must include the power to enable the person to believe in the first place or else man would never choose the good and always choose the evil (Jer. 13.23; Matt. 7.18; Jn. 3.3; Rom. 8.7-8).

Some time ago a friend of mine, who was attending seminary at the time, recounted the story of being in class with a student that was arguing and insisting that believers could lose their salvation. My good friend tried to show him how that would result in a lack of assurance, and rightly so. I suggested the proper answer would be that if we could lose salvation because of our own sin, than we are *surely* to be damned! Man simply does not have the goodness within himself to become saved and stay saved, it must be an all-grace-gospel, or it would cease to be good news. Hodge insisted on the same conclusion from his exposition of Romans 4.16:

> "If salvation be in any form or to any degree dependent on the merit, the goodness, or the stability of man, it never can be sure, nay, it must be utterly unattainable. Unless we are saved by grace, we cannot be saved at all. To reject, therefore a gratuitous salvation, is to reject the only method of salvation available for sinners."[59]

[59]Charles Hodge, *Romans, Geneva Series of Commentaries* (Edinburgh: Banner of Truth Trust, 2009) p.123.

Justification is about Peace

In order to appreciate the resultant peace of justification, several other precious and indispensable aspects of salvation must be highlighted. Peace with God has much more to do than simply our personal experience of that peace. Although a person who has gone from death to life and darkness to light through the cross of Jesus Christ can testify to the inner peace imparted at conversion; the peace which results from being accepted by God is much more profound than that. Although a person's emotional experience of God's peace may fluctuate with time and circumstance, God's peace remains a reality for the person who has been justified, however much he/she may no longer feel it. Peace with God is not simply a feeling, it is a fact.

Having peace with God results in man being joined to a right fellowship with God through reconciliation. The institution of familial ties through adoption, and the constitution of a new-found peace between Jew and Gentile through the church, are also a result of being in a peaceful relationship with God. The fascinating truth concerning all of these facets of salvation is that these are only possible through the cross. Only through the cross can man be at peace with God, only through the cross can the sinner be forgiven, and Jew and Gentile brought into fellowship as "one man." This is just another reason why we must never allow the center of our gospel to shift. Christ crucified must remain at the heart of our good news. The world is full of enmity, both between God and man, and man with himself. Only through the wrath-removing cross of Christ can sinners escape this enmity and dwell in peace.

Ephesians 2:11–19 [11] "Therefore remember that formerly you, the Gentiles in the flesh, who are called "Uncircumcision" by the so-called "Circumcision," which is performed in the flesh by human hands— [12] remember that you were at that time separate from Christ, excluded from the commonwealth of Israel, and strangers to the covenants of promise, having no hope and without God in the world. [13] But now in Christ Jesus you who formerly were far off have been brought near by the blood of Christ. [14] For He Himself is our peace, who made both groups into one and broke down the barrier of the dividing wall, [15] by abolishing in His flesh the enmity, which is the Law of commandments contained in ordinances, so that in Himself He might make the two into one new man, thus establishing peace, [16] and might reconcile them both in one body to God through the cross, by it having put to death the enmity. [17] And He came and preached peace to you who were far away, and peace to those who were near; [18] for through Him we both have our access in one Spirit to the Father. [19] So then you are no longer strangers and aliens, but you are fellow citizens with the saints, and are of God's household…"

Justification is about bringing an end to the deep-seated hostility between Jew and Gentile, but even more profound and more critical is the peace that reconciles God and man. The nature of this peace, however, is not easily understood. This peace has been equated with emotions and the *peace* we feel, a particular standard of living, material blessing, a tranquil and quiet life, and the experience derived through our personal devotion to God. But the peace that results from justification is above all a *forensic* peace, a relational peace, a peace that happens on a spiritual plane. In order to understand more fully the nature of this peace, we should focus on a few important aspects of salvation.

Peace and God's Wrath

Justification resolves our greatest of all dilemmas; sin and its consequences (cf. 1 Cor. 15.56). God takes away our enmity through propitiation. Propitiation was God's way of satisfying His just wrath.[60] He sent His Son publicly to do this very thing:

> **Romans 3:24–25** [24] "being justified as a gift by His grace through the redemption which is in Christ Jesus; [25] whom God displayed publicly as a propitiation in His blood through faith. This was to demonstrate His righteousness, because in the forbearance of God He passed over the sins previously committed."

The wrath of God was built up against us. As Robert Reymond has pointed out, "divine wrath" is the "presupposition" of what he called, "Christ's obedient cross-work of propitiation".[61] John Murray attests to

---

[60] For critical Scripture texts on the doctrine of Propitiation see: Rom. 3.25, Heb. 2.17, 1 John 2.2, 4.10. The meaning of the ($i\lambda\alpha\sigma\mu\acute{o}$ / $i\lambda\alpha\sigma\tau\acute{\eta}\rho\iota o\nu$) word-group can have both the connotation of placating or appeasing God's anger (propitiation) as well as the cancellation and removal of sin (expiation). The former is intended here, the latter will be emphasized below. For an excellent treatment of the word-group see, Leon Morris, *The Apostolic Preaching of the Cross.* (London: Tyndale, 1955).

[61] R. L. Reymond, A New Systematic Theology of the Christian Faith, p.635.

this as well, "Propitiation presupposes the wrath and displeasure of God, and the purpose of propitiation is the removal of this displeasure."[62] We see the effects of God's wrath in our world even now (Rom. 1.18), we ourselves were children of wrath (Eph. 2.3), we were under the wrath of God (Jn. 3.36), and we needed to be delivered from the wrath of God (Matt. 3.7). Propitiation is a doctrine which has all but disappeared from American pulpits. Churches do not preach about propitiation because they do not want to preach about the anger of God or the judgment of God. Regarding God's wrath, and the concept of eternal punishment in Hell, William Nichols rightly points out:

> "Modern evangelicals, although not denying the existence of hell, soften its terrors at every possible point, and even makes God look kinder and more acceptable to sinners, they presume that it overcomes much of the enmity that sinners have towards God, which may cause them to more readily accept Jesus as their Savior."[63]

Too often God's glory is maligned because of soft preaching that portrays God as a big pushover in the sky that will not get angry with anyone and certainly not send anyone to Hell for their sins. People speak of God's love to the exclusion of His wrath and in doing so we get only half the God. God's wrath, however, is rooted in His holiness (Is. 5.16; Ezek. 28.22; Rev. 6.10; 16.5). Because God is so holy, righteous, and true He does not tolerate contradictions to His perfections. Again Murray says,

> "Vengeance is the reaction of the holiness of God to sin, and the covering is that which provides for the removal of divine displeasure which the sin evokes."[64]

When Paul described the sinful nature of man he summed it up as the failure to measure up to God's glory or His perfections, "all have sinned and fall short of the glory of God" (Rom. 3.23). This is what God is so angry about, His glory has been contradicted by sin. His glory, as it was intended to be reflected by man, has been diminished by the wickedness of man who seeks his own glory rather than God's.

---

[62]Murray, *Redemption Accomplished and Applied*, p.30.

[63]William C. Nichols, *The Torments of Hell, Jonathan Edwards on Eternal Damnation.* (Iowa, International Outreach Inc., 2006) p.223.

[64]Murray, *Redemption Accomplished and Applied*, p.30.

When seen on the backdrop of man's sin, propitiation shines forth with precious glory. Being justified through the cross-work of Christ means that God's wrath concerning the perversion of His glory has been satisfied and removed from sinners. The hammer stroke of God's justice fell on the Son when it should have fallen on us and in so doing He took the full brunt of God's displeasure for sin. Although God would have been utterly just to punish all past sins, *previously committed*, He chose to show mercy on the vessels of mercy by sending His Son to take away the righteous anger of God. The blood of Jesus was shed to justify sinners and to appease the wrath of God which sinners have provoked in Him. Paul says this very thing to the Romans, later in the book:

> **Romans 5:6–9** [6] "For while we were still helpless, at the right time Christ died for the ungodly. [7] For one will hardly die for a righteous man; though perhaps for the good man someone would dare even to die. [8] But God demonstrates His own love toward us, in that while we were yet sinners, Christ died for us. [9] Much more then, having now been justified by His blood, we shall be saved from the wrath of God through Him."

The cross is a perpetual reminder that God's anger had to be averted if sinners were to experience the peace of God. This is crucial to the good news of the gospel and we dare not leave it out of our preaching. As we build the case for sin and its consequences we should be setting the stage for the wonder of propitiation. Propitiation is assumed in Paul's words in Romans 5.1, "Therefore, having been justified by faith, we have peace with God through our Lord Jesus Christ." The prepositional phrase, "through our Lord Jesus Christ" implies not only Christ as sin-bearing substitute, but Christ as our peace-making sacrifice.

The results of such a peace-making crucifixion are great in every way. From enemies to friends, from children of wrath to children of God, and from eternal punishment to eternal joy—propitiation has rendered God favorably disposed to us through Jesus Christ so that we become fellow heirs with Him (Rom. 8.17).

What marvelous and glorious news for sinners who fear God's wrath. Sinners are in bondage to fear (Heb. 2.14-15), they are afraid of death, afraid of the unknown, they fear the possibility of judgment, and some, the certainty of it. Preaching Christ crucified assures them that there is much to fear, but that there is much more to trust Christ for than merely a temporary good life now. The more of the infinite wrath they fear, the more of the infinite peace they need. When presented alongside of the teaching of propitiation, the gospel becomes manifestly good news. If preached correctly it can answer the objections to God's wrath because He is holy, God's punishment of sinners because of the perversion of God's glory, and the satisfaction of God's justice because of Christ's cross-work and His propitiating sacrifice.

Peace and God's Forgiveness

The glorious good news of forgiveness has fallen on hard times in our postmodern culture. Forgiveness has been reordered away from heaven and God and directed squarely upon the Humanist *self*. If man is the center and measure of all things, then the greatest thing of all is to forgive yourself, to heal yourself, to rehabilitate the self, to improve and empower the self because lost inside of the self are all of the powers for living the kind of life man was meant to live. Such views of man are what David Wells called, "alternative anthropologies"[65]; anthropologies which are inherently Humanistic, self -consciously relativistic, and unashamedly narcissistic. In the end, as Wells points out, we have new emerging concepts of who and what man is. In fact, because of the total reordering of morality and ethics David Wells sees a frightening development on human identity altogether. Wells says, "This is the situation that is assuming epidemic proportions in our postmodern world."[66]

Ironically, it is this very loss of identity to which Wells speaks, which has rendered the modern man incapable of connecting with the importance of justification. Because he has replaced guilt with shame, sin with sickness, and righteousness with self-esteem; man lacks the necessary basis with which he can appreciate the cleansing power of the cross, through justification and the forgiveness it brings. Preaching the justifying power of the cross and the forgiveness of sin is a unique opportunity to help man to see his true identity from a redemptive perspective.

As much as our postmodern culture attempts to suppress the truth of God, the concept of peace resonates with people—they understand peace in basic form just like they understand justice in basic form. God's

---

[65] Wells, *Losing our Virtue*, p.141.

[66] Ibid.

common grace has given man a conscience, a sense of morality, a basic knowledge of his creatureliness and his accountability before God (Rom. 1.18ff.). Even further is the reality that God has written "the work of the Law" on man's hearts so that they know not only that murder is wrong, but that they stand accountable for such things before their Maker who will judge them for their deeds (Rom. 2.14-15). As we have seen in chapter two, before we can present sinners with the precious truth about forgiveness we must make them sensible of their sin and misery through the Law and through the curse-bearing cross. As we do this, we can begin to preach the truth to them concerning who they are, why they exist, how to make sense of the world around them, and where they must go for answers if they are to have true peace in this life and in the world to come. Instead of an *alternative* anthropology, they will have biblical anthropology that understands rightly the *Creator/creature* distinction that alone can account for the way things work in God's world.

Justification produces peace because justification produces forgiveness. Instead of forgiving themselves, man must be forgiven by God, instead of achieving personal peace through coming to "accept who you are"—the sinner can only have peace through seeing himself as a sinner in need of forgiveness (cf. Lk. 18.13). Justification provides that forgiveness. Consequently, this forgiveness is essential to have peace with God. This message of forgiveness was at the very center of the apostolic message:

Acts 2:38 [38] "Peter said to them, "Repent, and each of you be baptized in the name of Jesus Christ for the forgiveness of your sins; and you will receive the gift of the Holy Spirit.

Acts 5:31 [31] "He is the one whom God exalted to His right hand as a Prince and a Savior, to grant repentance to Israel, and forgiveness of sins."

Acts 10:43 [43] "Of Him all the prophets bear witness that through His name everyone who believes in Him receives forgiveness of sins."

Acts 13:38 [38] "Therefore let it be known to you, brethren, that through Him forgiveness of sins is proclaimed to you…"

This last passage, from Acts 13, brings the cross back to the center. It is only *through Him*, that is, through the person and work of Jesus Christ that forgiveness of sins is possible. To be justified is to be put right with God. It is to have the offenses of our sins removed, expiated, and remitted. It is to have sin completely dealt with, Morris illustrates:

> "The righteousness we have is not our own, it comes as God's good gift in Christ. But we will be righteous. Notice that this means more than being pardoned. The pardoned criminal bears no penalty, but he bears a stigma. He is a criminal and he is known as a criminal, albeit an unpunished one. The justified sinner not only bears no penalty; he is righteous. He is not a man with his sin still about him. The effect of Christ's work is to remove his sin completely."[67]

No longer having our sins "about us" (especially positionally), we can be free from all guilt, even the memory of our guilt. Therefore, to be justified means that men can live with a clean conscience again a conscience that, like the psalmist, responds in praise for the purifying power of justification and forgiveness (Ps. 32. 1-2; Rom. 4.7-8). The conscience is a powerful thing. When the conscience is confronted by God's law, God's curse, and Christ's curse-bearing cross men's hearts are weighed down with conviction, with guilt, and with an overwhelming sense of the judgment incurred by sin (Rom. 2.15). But Christ came to cleanse man from his sin and thus from his sin-smitten conscience:

> **Hebrews 9:14** [14] "how much more will the blood of Christ, who through the eternal Spirit offered Himself without blemish to God, cleanse your conscience from dead works to serve the living God?"

> **Hebrews 10:22** [22] "let us draw near with a sincere heart in full assurance of faith, having our hearts sprinkled clean from an evil conscience and our bodies washed with pure water."

Regardless of how psychologically programmed our generation is regarding sin and guilt, no twelve step program can cleanse the internal abiding voice of conscience except God. The more man suppresses the truth of his/her conscience the more authenticity they will lack in their everyday lives and the louder conscience will preach! It was J.C. Ryle who said, "A peace of conscience not built upon justification is a perilous

---

[67]Morris, *The Cross in the New Testament*, p.247.

dream."[68] God's justifying grace forgives and cleanses us so that we can live lives of authentic praise and genuine love. Conscience carries with it a high accountability partner within, a voice that never ceases to testify, and the objective record keeper of our deeds. The Puritans were masters in conscience-theology. English Puritan Richards Sibbes once said, "Conscience is above me, and God is above conscience", thereby stressing the authority conscience carries being subject to God alone.[69] Summing up Puritan thoughts on conscience, Beeke and Jones write:

> "In short, the Puritans taught that the conscience functions as a spiritual nervous system, which uses guilt to inform us that something is wrong and needs correction. Failing to heed the warnings of conscience can only lead to the hardening or searing of the conscience which in the end will bring us to destruction."[70]

It is only through the blood of the cross that men and women can truly be liberated to live before God with a pure conscience, or what Paul often refers to as a *good conscience*; something he saw as priceless (Acts 23.1; 24.16; 2 Cor. 1.12; 1 Tim. 1.19; 2 Tim. 1.3). It is through the resurrection that we are justified and it is through the justifying resurrection of Jesus Christ that we are able to obtain a *good conscience* (1 Pet. 3.21) leading to holiness; as James White noted, "The heart that knows the price paid for its redemption does not seek to add to the cost."[71] Through justification the sinner can receive the necessary cleansing they need from the wickedness of their former ways leading to true sanctification. One important text from Paul reminds us of this very thing:

> **1 Corinthians 6:9–11** [9] "Or do you not know that the unrighteous will not inherit the kingdom of God? Do not be deceived; neither fornicators, nor idolaters, nor adulterers, nor effeminate, nor homosexuals, [10] nor thieves, nor the covetous, nor drunkards, nor revilers, nor swindlers, will inherit the kingdom of God. [11] Such were some of you; but you were washed, but you

---

[68] J.C. Ryle, cited in *God's Gospel of Grace*, p.159.

[69] Richard Sibbes, *Works of Richard Sibbes* (Carlisle: Banner of Truth, 2001) 3.210.

[70] Joel R. Beeke & Mark Jones, *A Puritan Theology: Doctrine for Life* (Grand Rapids: Reformation Heritage Books, 2012) p.912.

[71] James R. White, *The God Who Justifies* (Minneapolis: Bethany House, 2001) p.100.

were sanctified, but you were justified in the name of the Lord Jesus Christ and in the Spirit of our God."

Justification affords the sinner many precious promises: a right standing with God, the imputation of Christ's righteousness, our adoption into God's family, and the focus here, the fact that God will not deal with sinners according to their God provoking sins. As Charles Hodge stated, the justified person has the promise that "in justification the believer receives the promise that God will not deal with him according to his transgressions."[72] All of God's promises are affirmed in Christ (2 Cor. 1.20). The promise of the forgiveness of sin resulting in peace is magnificent in every way. To be crucified for our peace means Jesus was crucified to put us right with God, to deliver us from the just wrath of God, to redeem us from the curse of God's law, and to cleanse us through the regenerating work of the Spirit of God by washing our sins away and granting us a pure conscience before God and man so that in the world and in the church we can invoke a good conscience to testify to our holiness and godly sincerity (2 Cor. 1.12). While the Law demands justification, the cross-work of Christ provides it. Justification is just another reason why we must keep Christ crucified at the center of our evangelism and preaching. Therefore, we cannot fail to preach the grace of justification. As we saw above, justification is about grace—is it any wonder then that Paul should magnify the grace of God, as the cross-work of Christ, which results in our redemption and forgiveness?:

> **Ephesians 1:7–8** [7] "In Him we have redemption through His blood, the forgiveness of our trespasses, according to the riches of His grace [8] which He lavished on us. In all wisdom and insight..."

---

[72]Charles Hodge, vol. 3, *Systematic Theology*, 164.

4

CRUCIFIED IN OUR PLACE, PREACHING THE MERCY OF SUBSTITUTIONARY ATONEMENT

"There is no one of the titles of Christ which is more precious to Christian hearts than "Redeemer"… It gives expression not merely to our sense that we have received salvation from Him, but also to our appreciation of what it cost Him to procure this salvation for us. It is the name specifically of the Christ of the cross. Whenever we pronounce it, the cross is placarded before our eyes and our hearts are filled with loving remembrance not only that Christ has given us salvation, but that He paid a mighty price for it."[73]

— B.B. Warfield

Christ *crucified* is the acorn of the mighty oak of God's sovereign grace. It is the fount from whence all redemptive blessings flow, every concentric and theological thought intersects on the cross. The phrase *Christ crucified* has a definite gravity about it, so that departing from Paul's *determination* is to depart from the Christ centered gospel, which was not only entrusted to him, but to which he himself was resolutely devoted. The concept of the substitutionary atonement of Christ is part of this glorious gospel apex which we are to preach. As Packer rightly noted, "This notion [i.e. of substitutionary atonement] takes us to the very heart of the Christian gospel."[74] Christ crucified for sinners can never be abandoned and must be understood if we would preach Christ to the glory of God. Paul resonated with this substitutionary as-

---

[73]B.B. Warfield, *The Works of Benjamin B. Warfield* (Grand Rapids: Baker Book House Company, 2003) vol. II, p.375.

[74]J.I. Packer, *What Did The Cross Achieve? The Logic of Penal Substitution.* Tyndale Bulletin vol. 25 (1974) p.4. [Brackets and italics mine].

pect of the cross when he told the Galatians he would never set it aside for his own sake:

> **Galatians 2:20–21** [20] "I have been crucified with Christ; and it is no longer I who live, but Christ lives in me; and the life which I now live in the flesh I live by faith in the Son of God, who loved me and gave Himself up for me. [21] I do not nullify the grace of God, for if righteousness comes through the Law, then Christ died needlessly."

Galatians, particularly (3:10-14), gives us a good starting point for the doctrine which is often called, *the penal substitutionary atonement of Christ*.[75] We see three things from this critical passage in Galatians 3: the need for atonement because of the curse of the Law, how the curse is removed, and the saving effects of the curse-exchange.

The Curse of the Law

We have already seen (in chapter two of this volume) how Paul's argument for Christ's *vicarious*[76] work takes shape. Man is unbearably lost, burdened, and condemned under the weight of the Law's demands. Judaizers, attempting to use the Law as a means to be justified in God's sight were drawing the Galatians away to another, manifestly, false gospel (Gal. 1.6-9). The justified man is to live by faith (3.11). Since faith alone can justify, law-keeping is excluded by the gospel. The person attempting to gain his right standing before God through law-keeping was under the misery of an unbearable burden; Paul, quoting Deuteronomy 27.26, says, "for it is written, "Cursed is everyone who does not abide by all things written in the book of the law, to perform them" (Gal. 3.10).

It is precisely this *curse*[77] that Paul sees as the sinner's greatest dilemma. Bearing in mind that, especially in the OT context in which this curse was

---

[75] So for example, Berkhof, "the penal substitutionary doctrine of atonement": *Systematic Theology*, 1996; p.373ff. See also Bavinck who says, "Christ's entire life and work, from his conception to this death, was substitutionary in nature." *Reformed Dogmatics*, vol. 3 p. 378.

[76] Often used in place of *substitutionary* language; "vicar" meaning someone who takes the place of another or a representative. See, Grudem's, *Systematic Theology* (Leicester, England; Grand Rapids, MI: Zondervan 2004) p.579.

[77] *Κατάρα*: a covenantal term that is part of the stipulations of the Mosaic covenant of Sinai (Deut. 28-32; Lev. 26).

introduced, and as Gal. 3.13 goes on to flesh out, the curse was a public display of God's displeasure of condemned criminals who had transgressed His Law.[78] Commentators have often pointed out this background:

> "Hanging was not a method of execution, but something that was done after the death of a criminal, on the same day. When the man was dead, he would be hanged on a tree or a 'wooden post' of some kind; the gruesome sight would then serve as a warning to the population of the results of breaking those laws which were punishable by death."[79]

We should point out, as does Schreiner,[80] that being put on a tree was not automatically or universally indicative of God's curse, since so many Christians were themselves crucified for their faith in Christ. Still, the burden of the curse makes clear one thing; those who stand under the shadow of it are incapable of freeing themselves from it, they must do "all things written in the book of the Law" (3.11b). Although Deuteronomy 27.26 does not specify the word *all*,[81] chapter 28 makes it clear that "everything" or "all" that is commanded was to be kept perfectly (28.1). While this curse is the logical outcome of breaking God's Law, the gospel of grace takes us in a totally different direction. The Law in this context condemns (2 Cor. 3.6-7, 9), the gospel gives life, "in Jesus Christ" (Rom. 6.23). Thus, the Law in the context of Galatians shows our absolute need for the righteousness of Christ— a righteousness made possible only by His blood-covenant (cf. 2 Cor. 3.9).[82] In his response to N.T. Wright, Piper comments and rightly interprets Galatians 3:

> "The law, in this narrow, short-term design, demands perfectly doing the 613 commandments of the Pentateuch in order to

---

[78]This also reinforces our earlier notion that the cross produces a unique guilt or awareness of one's sin and miserable condition before God.

[79]Peter C. Craigie, *The Book of Deuteronomy*, New International Commentary on the Old Testament (Grand Rapids: Eerdmans, 1976), 285; as cited in: Thomas R. Schreiner, *Galatians, Zondervan Exegetical Commentary on the New Testament* (Grand Rapids, MI: Zondervan, 2010), pp.216-17.

[80]Schreiner, *Galatians, Zondervan Commentary on the New Testament*, p.217.

[81]Heb: כל. "all". This also had to be done with "caution" שמר.

[82]The "condemnation" ($\kappa\alpha\tau\acute{\alpha}\kappa\rho\iota\sigma\iota\varsigma$) / "righteousness" ($\delta\iota\kappa\alpha\iota\sigma\sigma\acute{\upsilon}\nu\eta$) contrast between the two covenants (or as Paul refers to them "ministries") makes clear what each covenant produces i.e. either condemnation leading to death or righteousness leading to life.

have life... This is not a kind of legal arrangement that excludes reliance on God for enabling power. There is no thought in this arrangement of man being required to give to God what he has not first given to man (Rom. 11:35-36). This narrow, short-term design of the law holds up an absolute standard of child-like, humble, God-reliant, God exalting perfection, and thus produced the moral backdrop without which the sin-atoning provision of the Pentateuch and the work of Christ would make no sense."[83]

It is precisely the extensive demands of the Law that makes Christ's atonement so necessary and so precious. At the very bottom of it, the gospel is about rescue, relief, and respite for the weary sinner who is mercilessly enslaved to his own devices through sin. The Law explains the nature of this dilemma and multiplies its sinfulness, it *increases* sin (cf. Rom. 5.20) and thus, increases the burden of the curse-incurring Law. It becomes critical therefore that this curse be removed if man is to be freed from its consequences and liberated from its tyranny over his life.

How the Curse is Removed

I will never forget watching a sad press conference in 2010 when Tiger Woods made his public apology for his now infamous marital scandal. He seemed contrite, tired, angry, awkward and overwhelmed. What stuck out to me from Woods' apology were the words, "I have a lot of atoning to do." As a self-proclaimed Buddhist, Tiger's religion has no concept of atonement plus, the only atonement which could actually remove his guilty stains is not something he could perform. Although he sees his need for atonement and some way to erase the mistakes, the shame, and the guilt of his sins, the famed Pro golfer like every other son or daughter of Adam stands powerless to make such an atonement for sin. What else could we call this condition but a curse! But atonement itself must be made if sinners will be put right with God. As is often the case, the Bible's teaching on atonement leads in the direction of substitution. Biblical scholarship often points this out:

"The sins of humanity violated the holiness of the Creator and brought the sentence of death, a sentence that can be averted

---

[83]John Piper, *The Future of Justification, A Response to N.T. Wright* (Wheaton: Crossway Books, 2007) p. 197

only by the substitution of a sacrifice of death. Through the blood of sacrifice, sinful people are able to receive the blessing of God instead of his judgment."[84]

The sinner's plight under the curse of the Law leaves the sinner in a vacuous condition of hopelessness. Although the natural man left to himself cannot see his own condition, his conscience and God's Word make it clear that he is under a curse nonetheless (Rom. 2.14ff). Arising out of man's dim condition is the question of *liberation*. How is man to be freed from this curse and how does it work; which is to ask, how does God do it? How does God free people who are under such an incredible burden and who are powerless to deliver themselves from the impending judgment of God's wrath being guilty of breaking God's commands? According to Paul, Christ bears our curse. Christ came to do what we could not do; both to fulfill the legal demands of the Law (Christ's active obedience) and absorb the Law's awful penalty (passive obedience) for those who were impotent to do so; Paul says, "While we were still helpless… Christ died for the ungodly" (Rom. 5.6). Anthony Hoekema points out this very thing:

> "That Christ was our substitute is taught with inescapable clarity and force in Galatians 3:13, "Christ redeemed us form the curse of the law by becoming a curse for us (*hyper hēmōn*)."[85] We deserved that curse, since we do not and cannot obey God's law perfectly (vv.10-11). But Christ bore the curse in our stead, as our substitute, even becoming a curse for us, so that we might be delivered from it."[86]

Several years ago, I was involved in a convalescent home ministry in Southern California where our church reached out to the elderly who were unable to go to church. The home was filled with unique and interesting people from every walk of life. One dear lady in particular always stood out to me, she claimed to be a believer and would often

---

[84]Leland Ryken, James C. Wilhoit, Tremper Longman III, *The Dictionary of Biblical Imagery* (Downers Grove: IVP Academic, 1998) p.54.

[85]The full phrase, Χριστὸς ἡμᾶς ἐξηγόρασεν ἐκ τῆς κατάρας τοῦ νόμου γενόμενος ὑπὲρ ἡμῶν κατάρα (Gal. 3.13a). The prepositional phrase (ὑπὲρ ἡμῶν) is not only the object of the circumstantial participle but also indicates advantage i.e. of believers.

[86]Anthony Hoekema, *Saved by Grace* (Grand Rapids, MI; Cambridge, UK: Eerdmans 1994) p.174.

go on and on about growing up in the church as a little girl. I would often ask her if she was praying, reading her Bible, and attending Bible study at the convalescent home whenever a minister came to share the Word with them. Her response was always the same, "Not as much as I should." In fact every time I visited her, I would ask the same questions and get the same answer, "Have you been reading your Bible?" her response, "Not as much as I should", "Have you been spending any time in prayer", again, "Not as much as I should." The script was always the same. The difference between this dear old saint, if in fact she was a saint, and the sinner outside of Christ is that for the unbeliever, his failure to fulfill what God's Word demands places him/her under a curse, not with regard to missing the mark in sanctification, but of a sure condemnation for falling short of the glory of God. Regardless of the effort, if our deeds are not *exceeding the righteousness of the Pharisees* we will surely fall short!

No matter how many good deeds a sinner might perform there will always be more to do, he will never have done *as much as he should.* He not only has the deeds themselves to perform, but they must also be done with pure motives and to the glory of God. Having no capacity to fulfill all that the Law demands, Jesus "bore the curse in our stead"[87] (v.11b) and not by law-keeping. This makes it *evident* that man cannot be justified by the works of the Law (v.11a). Faith and works are incompatible with one another as far as our justification is concerned (Gal. 2.16). Christ went so far as to *become* a curse to redeem us and rescue us and deliver us *from* the curse. Christ came near to the curse to remove us far from it, He bore the curse so that we no longer had to be under its condemnation. Motivated solely by His sovereign mercy, God sent us a Deliverer who would free us from our oppression and despair by taking our place (cf. Jn.15.13). He was put to shame so that we could be vindicated. He humbled Himself so that we could be exalted. This is how, as God's Servant, Christ has *healed us*:

> **Isaiah 53:4–6** [4] "Surely our griefs He Himself bore, And our sorrows He carried; Yet we ourselves esteemed Him stricken, Smitten of God, and afflicted. [5] But He was pierced through for our transgressions, He was crushed for our iniquities; The chas-

---

[87]NKJV.

tening for our well-being fell upon Him, And by His scourging we are healed. ⁶ All of us like sheep have gone astray, Each of us has turned to his own way; But the Lord has caused the iniquity of us all To fall on Him."

Isaiah 53:10–11 ¹⁰ "But the Lord was pleased To crush Him, putting Him to grief; If He would render Himself as a guilt offering, He will see His offspring, He will prolong His days, And the good pleasure of the Lord will prosper in His hand. ¹¹ As a result of the anguish of His soul, He will see it and be satisfied; By His knowledge the Righteous One, My Servant, will justify the many, As He will bear their iniquities."

As we preach Christ crucified we awaken sinners to the plight of sin and the dread of God's penal curse. Preaching Christ crucified also must involve the marvelous work of the Redeemer who gave Himself as that infinite costly sacrifice as payment for the debt of our sin— a debt beyond all human merit. Redemption is how God delivers us from the curse and makes us right with Him. The word *to redeem* ($\dot{\varepsilon}\xi\alpha\gamma o\rho\dot{\alpha}\zeta\omega$) in Galatians 3.13 means literally "to buy back, to deliver, to set free, to release". Louw and Nida's Lexicon define the word as causing "the release or freedom of someone by a means which proves costly to the individual causing the release."[88] In order for Christ to redeem us, however, He had to step into our place. As Paul put it, "He made Him who knew no sin *to be* sin on our behalf, so that we might become the righteousness of God in Him" (2 Cor. 5. 21), to be numbered with sinners (Is. 53.12; Lk. 22.37), to give His life as a ransom for many (Mt. 20.28), to allow the life of His blood to flow freely to us (Lev. 17.11; Jn. 6.53), and to refuse any other way of obtaining the purchased possession (Mt. 26.39; Heb. 12.2), voluntarily He went to the cross to make such a substitutionary atonement for all of God's elect people (cf. Jn. 10.11; Acts 20.28; Heb. 2.10-13) so that not one of them would ever be lost (Jn. 10.27-29; 17.12):

Luke 22:19–20 ¹⁹ "And when He had taken some bread and given thanks, He broke it and gave it to them, saying, "This is My body which is given for you; do this in remembrance of Me." ²⁰

---

[88]Johannes P. Louw and Eugene Albert Nida, vol. 1, *Greek-English Lexicon of the New Testament: Based on Semantic Domains*, electronic ed. of the 2nd edition. (New York: United Bible Societies, 1996), 487.

And in the same way He took the cup after they had eaten, saying, "This cup which is poured out for you is the new covenant in My blood."[89]

The Saving Effects of the Curse-Exchange

We should say one more thing concerning the Galatians 3 text; namely that such a great salvation has many important and redemptive after effects. Because of the great curse-exchanging work of Christ's substitutionary atoning death on the cross, Paul returns once again to the theme of redemptive blessing.

Every time we preach Christ correctly and sinners come to know the merciful love of the Savior, we enter the stream of God's redemptive mission and work, which began ages ago and is now being supremely revealed through Jesus Christ (cf. Eph. 3.1-12). Notice how for Paul, speaking about the covenant at Sinai, the Law, the curse and its remedy results in redemption and in moving backwards another four hundred years in redemptive history to Abraham. Paul opened up this entire section by focusing on faith and arguing from Abraham (Gal. 3.6-9). Upon dealing with the Judaizers and their insistence on Law-keeping, Paul refutes them with the overwhelming, obligatory curse-inducing nature of the Law, thereby demonstrating that works and faith are incompatible (vv.10-13). Paul magnifies the substitutionary work of the Redeemer, who took the curse in our place, thereby redeeming us from the curse of the Law (v.13). Paul now returns to the importance of connecting us to the faith of Abraham and the blessing of being children of Abraham through faith (v.7).

In verse 14, Paul focuses on two effects of the curse-exchange, the covenant of Abraham, and the promise of the Spirit.

The Covenant of Abraham

We could say that the worst curse imaginable paved the way to the greatest blessing conceivable. Those who were outside of the sphere of God's blessings are brought near by Christ and blessed in fulfillment of the Covenant promises made to Abraham (cf. Eph. 2.11ff). This blessing is the fulfillment of the promise made to Abraham and repeated to his descendants throughout the Patriarchal period in Genesis:

---

[89]Emphasis mine.

Genesis 12:1–3 [1] "Now the Lord said to Abram, "Go forth from your country, And from your relatives And from your father's house, To the land which I will show you; [2] And I will make you a great nation, And I will bless you, And make your name great; And so you shall be a blessing; [3] And I will bless those who bless you, And the one who curses you I will curse. And in you all the families of the earth will be blessed.""

Genesis 18:18 [18] "since Abraham will surely become a great and mighty nation, and in him all the nations of the earth will be blessed?"

Genesis 22:18 [18] "In your seed all the nations of the earth shall be blessed, because you have obeyed My voice."

Genesis 26:4 [4] "I will multiply your descendants as the stars of heaven, and will give your descendants all these lands; and by your descendants all the nations of the earth shall be blessed…"

Genesis 28:14 [14] "Your descendants will also be like the dust of the earth, and you will spread out to the west and to the east and to the north and to the south; and in you and in your descendants shall all the families of the earth be blessed."

This promise, however, was realized in Abraham's one and ultimate descendent, namely Christ. The purpose of the curse-exchange, therefore, was to bring salvation to all of the nations of the earth. The blessing is global in its scope and it was to be comprised of *all nations*.[90] However, this multi-national group is said to be blessed in connection to Abraham somehow. The promise is clear, the blessing is "in you" (Gen. 12.3), but later the promise is made more specific to mean that the promises were made to Abraham and to his "seed"[91] (Gen. 22.18). The promise was indeed made to Abraham because he was the archetype of faith, "Abraham the believer" (Gal. 3.9). But the promise was also to be understood through his typological *seed* which Paul plainly identifies as Jesus, "and to your seed," that is, Christ"[92] (Gal. 3.16). This is yet another example

---

[90]Cf. Rev. 5.9-10.

[91]Note the use of the singular: זרע.

[92]The full phrase is: *Καὶ τῷ σπέρματί σου ἐστιν Χριστός.*

of how God binds the entire panoply of Scripture together with all of its shadows, types, prophecies and promises around the person and work of Jesus Christ (cf. 2 Cor. 1.20). As the great 19th century English Puritan expositor John Brown noted, there can be no doubt that Abraham's promise was to be ultimately conceived along Messianic lines:

> "There is no doubt that this is the fact—that in the promise, "In thy Seed shall all the families of the earth be blessed," the reference is not to the descendants of Abraham generally, nor to his descendants by Isaac, nor to his spiritual descendants, but to his great descendant, the Messiah."[93]

The curse-exchanging work of the promised *Seed* results in the benefits that flow to us through the fulfillment of the promise. Because we are united to the Seed, Christ brings the blessings that belonged to Abraham to us. This is why Paul can say, "… those who are of faith are blessed *with*[94] Abraham, the believer" (Gal. 3.9). Furthermore, the future Mosaic covenant does not invalidate this previous Abrahamic covenant so that we are not bound to Law-keeping as a means of obtaining God's justifying grace (Gal. 3.15-18). Through faith in the *Seed* we are now connected to the promise of the covenant made with Abraham. This connection is what theologians call, *Union with Christ*. The believer being united to Christ, one with Christ, connected to Christ, joined with Christ, and indeed *in Christ* through faith is the basis for making the believer the recipient of every conceivable spiritual blessing (Eph. 1.3-4). We should never think that any good thing comes to us from God apart from Christ. Neither in ministry, marriage, family or personal sanctification; whether we are speaking of some aspect of salvation like election, adoption, justification or glorification—Christ alone is the Benefactor of all Christian blessings whatever they may be. Such a glorious redemption is unending. As Berkhof states, "God appointed a vicar in Jesus Christ to take man's place, and this vicar atoned for sin and obtained an eternal *redemption* for man."[95] Consequently, we are now freed from the curse of the Law and

---

[93]John Brown, *Galatians*, p.144.

[94]Note the prepositional phrase in the verse: ὥστε οἱ ἐκ πίστς εὐλγοῦνται σὺν τῷ πιστῷ Ἀβραάμ. We are associated with Abraham primarily along *pistic* lines. Therefore, aside from physical descent, the crucial thing is a person's *faith* not bloodline.

[95]Louis Berkhof, *Systematic Theology* (Grand Rapids, MI / Cambridge, UK: Eerdmans Publishing, 1996) p.375. (Emphasis mine).

have now received the promise of the Spirit all because there was a substitute, a curse-bearer, and a curse-exchange resulting in our permanent justification before God.

The Promise of the Spirit

Another after effect of the curse-reversing cross-work of Christ was the promise of the Spirit (Gal. 3.14). Consequent to the work of Christ on the cross is the work of the Spirit in the believer. Christ having justified us by His death and redeemed us through His blood now gives us His Spirit as a pledge of great things (2 Cor. 1.21-22; Eph. 1.14). The Spirit is a *promissory* Spirit. He comes to us based upon great and magnificent promises and His presence among us and in us brings promises of greater things still (cf. Rom. 8.23). He is the promise of a sanctified life (Tit. 3.5), He is the promise of a life being led by God (Gal. 5.16), He is the assurance of God's unfailing fatherly love (Rom. 8.15-16), He is the Prosecutor of the world's sin and guilt attending our witness (Jn. 16.8-11), He is the promise of liberation and transformation (2 Cor. 3.17-18), and He is the down payment of our future redemption and glory (Eph. 4.30). This is the nature and character of the Spirit promised to us in the Abrahamic covenant finally realized in Christ.

Paul's point here is that the blessing of Abraham now comes to believers, whether Jew or Gentile, by faith. The phrase, "the promise of the Spirit" (Gal. 3.14a) is thus functioning as something of a synonym with "the blessing of Abraham" in (Gal. 3.14b). Because Christ became our substitute that takes away the wrath of God incurred by breaking God's curse-producing Law, believers receive the gift and promise of the Spirit by faith. Once again, as is the case throughout Galatians, this removes works as the basis for acceptance before God (cf. Gal. 2.16). Christ's substitutionary atonement is the path of blessing—the inheritance of very old and yet ever precious promises. Sinners should be made to see that apart from Christ stepping in as their substitute they will remain unblessed, children of the flesh and not children of promise, abandoned and accursed children instead of adopted and beloved children of God. Through the Abrahamic promise we inherit the earth (Rom. 4.13). But only through the curse-bearing Redeemer can we inherit any of God's redemptive promises (2 Cor. 1.20). This is why the cross must remain central to our message and uppermost in our preaching, for it was upon the cross that the vicarious Lamb of God came to lay down His life for

His sheep and secure their everlasting redemption; a redemption applied to them through the promised Holy Spirit.

The Absolute Necessity for a Substitute

So crucial, to the context of Galatians is the argument which assures Gentiles equal covenant status as Jews. Gentiles, like Jews, are justified and blessed, indeed "sons of Abraham" (Gal. 3.7) who have been "blessed with Abraham, the believer" (Gal 3.9). This means that all people are afforded this great Abrahamic blessing in the gospel regardless of race, nationality, ethnicity, gender, appearance, or social status. Preaching Christ crucified is a message of full acceptance. In fact, it is the only place to find acceptance with God. God has not made any other way for people to have their sins removed than through the substitute He Himself provided in Christ. It is only through this sacrifice that sinners have the potential for unspeakable gains and imperishable blessings. The Lord Jesus Christ must be set forth as a substitute with a purpose—He is the Hero indeed, the Savior-Lord of the world because He dies for the sin of the world (cf. Jn. 1.29; 1 Tim. 4.10). Regardless of whatever misconceptions people may have in mind when they reflect upon a substitutionary death, we must declare the whole counsel of God to them. Without the mercy of Christ's substitutionary death we fail to explain how God's righteous indignation and wrath is absorbed and sins removed from us.

The entire history of the Old Testament is a prefiguring of the absolute necessity for Christ's atoning glory. The Old Testament economy is full of Christological imagery which typologically speaks of Christ substitutionary work: God's sacrifice when He skins an animal to cover the shame of Adam and Eve (Gen. 3.21), Abraham's sacrifice of his only son Isaac (Gen. 22), the Servant of the Lord in Isaiah who voluntarily gives up his life for the sake of the many who are healed through him (Is. 53), etc. Perhaps nothing so pervasively prefigured the sacrifice of Christ on the cross than the Day of Atonement when the covenant people of God were corporately and ceremonially cleansed of sin. Hoekema writes:

> "The Day of Atonement was the high point of Old Testament worship; the sacrifices offered on that day for the sins of the people were uniquely prefigurative of Christ. The blood of the goat of the sin-offering was sprinkled on the mercy seat in order

to take away the sins of the people. When Paul says that God presented Christ as a hilastērion, he means that through the substitutionary sacrifice of Christ on the cross God's wrath against our sin has been averted and our guilt has been removed."[96]

Speaking about the rituals associated with the Day of Atonement, Gane's commentary agrees with Hoekema's assessment, "These rituals found fulfillment in our most holy Purification Offering (1 Jn. 1.29), who paradoxically allowed sin and death to penetrate him (2 Cor. 5.21) so that he can cleanse these evils out of those who accept his sacrifice."[97] Also, Steven Lawson points out that this day was pointing forward to the scapegoat character of Christ's offering on the cross:

> "When the high priest laid both of his hands upon the scapegoat and confessed the sins of the nation, the gesture represented a symbolic transfer of the sins of the people to this innocent sacrifice. The goat then was released into the wilderness, symbolically carrying the people's sins far away from them. This annual ritual prefigured the death of Christ for the sins of His people—for their sins to Him, and He carried them far away."[98]

Therefore, preaching Christ means that we explain the meaning of the dual aspect of the atonement, namely expiation and propitiation. Christ's death being, not simply about a divine love story, but the redemptive storyline of Scripture that explains how the awful wrath of God can be averted and how His awesome promises are received. This is why Morris says, "Christ's sacrifice has transformed the whole method of approach to God."[99] Whatever needed to be done in order to rid God's people of their sin has been exhaustively accomplished on the cross, "whatever needed to be done He [Christ] has done, fully, finally."[100] Being so incredibly competent as our priest-sacrifice who, unlike all previous priests (high priests or otherwise), Jesus needed no self-cleansing, no garments for purifica-

---

[96]Anthony Hoekema, *Saved by Grace*; p. 158.

[97]Roy Gane, *The NIV Application Commentary, Leviticus, Numbers* (Grand Rapids: Zondervan, 2004) p. 279.

[98]Steven J. Lawson, *Foundations of Grace, A Long Line of Godly Men*, vol.1 p. 88.

[99]Leon Morris, *The Cross in the New Testament*; p. 293. Morris is reflecting on the sacrifice of Christ in the book of Hebrews, see esp. pp.270-308 in the same volume.

[100]Ibid, p. 301.

tion, no special consecration for making Him ceremonially clean; Jesus was Himself "unblemished and spotless" (1 Pet. 1.19).

Sermons have often stressed the excellencies of Christ's sacrifice precisely on this point:

> "Jesus Christ is the One to whom all the priests beforehand pointed: the One who is holy, blameless, and pure; the One who is qualified to sacrifice "once for all" with the offering of his own blood; the One who is able to redeem us form sin and reconcile us to God."[101]

The mercy of substitution is in what it accomplishes and in what it reveals. Christ's substitutionary death procures all of God's blessings (Eph. 1.3; 2 Pet. 1.3-4) and reveals and accounts for the confirmation of all of God's redemptive promises (2 Cor. 1.20). The cross explains why an ancient promise made to an insignificant Mesopotamian pagan has any meaning for the 21st century man. Jesus redeems man from the terror of the curse and blesses him with the treasure of inheriting the earth! Christ's substitutionary death puts the glorious grace and love of God on display, not simply because Christ died, but because having died in our place He accomplishes so much for our everlasting good. Clinton Arnold said:

> "The ultimate demonstration of love is Jesus' act of laying down his life for his people to procure their forgiveness of sins and bring them into a relationship with God. His willing sacrifice serves as the hallmark example defining what it truly means to love."[102]

Christ's substitutionary sacrifice means that He courageously stood in our place. The love of Christ is displayed in His redemptive courage. The wrath, which was so imminently ready to break in upon us, was absorbed by the courage of the Son. He did not despise the shame, He did not refuse the Father's will, He did not ask to come down from the cross, knowing that dying for the sins of His people would result in the greatest display of God's glory and the greatest interest for securing the good of

---

[101]Richard D. Phillips, *Hebrews, Reformed Expository Commentary* (Phillipsburg: P&R Publishing, 2006) p. 263.

[102]Clinton E. Arnold, *Ephesians, Zondervan Exegetical Commentary on the New Testament* (Grand Rapids, MI: Zondervan, 2010), p. 311.

His people. Like the Old Testament goats (Lev. 16.6-10), part of Christ's sacrifice removed the wrath of God through propitiation, the other removed the presence and power of sin through expiation. Thus, to preach Christ crucified is inextricably annexed to the concepts of wrath satisfied and sin severed—two precious elements of the gospel message sinners so desperately need proclaimed and explained to them plainly and carefully. Above all, we do this by pointing them to the Savior's work on the cross saying, "…behold the Lamb of God that takes away the sin of the world."

5

CRUCIFIED TO SET US APART, PREACHING THE POWER OF THE CROSS TO SANCTIFY SINNERS

Preaching the cross is to preach God's purposes. The aim of the cross is to redeem a people who reflect God's moral perfections. The purpose is to restore the image of God in man so that what was lost may be recovered. Sin caused the contradiction of the glory of God in man (see Chapter Two). The redemption of the cross corrects this contradiction in us and restores us to the place where we rightly glorify God by reflecting in ourselves who God is. However, the cross is not simply the way to see God's purposes accomplished it is also the means through which God's purposes are applied to unworthy sinners. Sanctification is set in motion by the cross-work of Christ. For this reason the apostle Paul did not come preaching moral rehabilitation or ethical reform because this could not sanctify the hearts of God's people—he preached Christ crucified. The cross does not simply reform, but conforms (Rom. 8.29; 2 Cor. 3.18). Only the cross and the redemption that it brings has the power to sanctify the people of God.

In order for us to fully appreciate the necessity of preaching the cross' power to sanctify, we need to ask fundamental questions regarding the doctrine of sanctification itself and how it relates to what God has done through the cross. With worldliness at an all time high in the Church we need to ask how sinners can be set free from the power of the world's draw to sinful living. After all, what is going to sever the root of sin when a person has been living in it for so long, and what is going to sustain a person's passion for holiness all the life long, and how does the cross inform all of this? These are questions that must be explored if we, like Paul, are going to believe in the efficacy of the cross over other alternative, however relevant, means of setting forth Jesus Christ before unbelievers so as to win them to Him. We should also point out the cross' effects beyond justification; the doctrine most often associated with the cross. The cross, however, touches upon every aspect of salvation from election to glorification, the sufferings and subsequent glories of the cross are far reaching and immensely practical. The cross affects our redemption in that it is through the cross that we find ourselves justified before God (Rom. 5.9), it is through the cross that we are forgiven and reconciled to God (Eph. 1.7; Col. 1.20), we are adopted as children of God (Gal. 4.5), and we are also decisively set apart or sanctified definitively (Heb. 10.10). Yet, because our sanctification is not simply a matter of definitive sanctification our *progressive* sanctification is also *cruciform* in nature (cf. Jn. 21.19, 22).

The cross is not only the bridge that reconciles us to God it is furthermore the instrument upon which our lives are conformed into greater Christ-likeness on a daily basis (cf. 1 Pet. 2.21-25). To live a cross-centered life is to live in light of the cross, by the salvation wrought at the cross, by the grace given through the cross, and on the basis of the righteousness merited upon the cross. Therefore, to preach the cross is to preach the power of God, not only to justify sinners, but also to sanctify us for a lifetime. Preaching Christ crucified and risen again is to preach a message about a lifetime commitment to live holy in the Son of God, that is the cost. The cross carries a cost, a very big cost as we will see below. Thus, first and foremost we must begin with the demands of the cross to sanctity (i.e. to live godly, holy), to be willing to suffer as Christ did to be willing to undergo our own agonies and sufferings under the weight of our own crosses. John Piper speaks about the demands of the cross and its implications for Christian participation and suffering:

> "So he "set his face to go to Jerusalem" (Lk. 9.51). And he knew exactly what would happen there. It was all planned by his Father when he sent him into the world. "See, we are going up to Jerusalem, and the Son of Man will be delivered over to the chief priests and to scribes, and they will condemn him to death and deliver him over to the Gentiles. And they will mock him and spit on him, and flog him and kill him. And after three days he will rise" (Mark 10:33-34). That's the plan—down to the details of being spit on. That was the design of his life. And he knew that his own pain would also fall on those who followed him." [103]

---

[103] John Piper, *What Jesus Demands from the World* (Wheaton: Crossway Books, 2006) p. 70.

It is no wonder that after years of sanctification and seeing sanctification in others, sanctification has often been described in ways which make it seem more like suffering than sanctification. Such a universal ecclesiastical experience however is not without biblical warrant. If we think of suffering when we think of sanctification it's because these two realities are likewise linked in Scripture. Notice how Paul links the motif in Romans 8:

> **Romans 8:16–17** [16] "The Spirit Himself testifies with our spirit that we are children of God, [17] and if children, heirs also, heirs of God and fellow heirs with Christ, if indeed we suffer with Him so that we may also be glorified with Him."

Paul's reference to suffering did not spring into mind vacuously, there is a context. In verse 13 Paul has already spoken about suffering and sanctification when he said, "for if you are living according to the flesh, you must die; but if by the Spirit you are putting to death the deeds of the body, you will live." Here, *death* captures the essence of sanctification. Paul elaborates on this repeatedly in his letters where we find for example, Paul making the resolution to suffer with Christ as part of his union with Christ, "that I may know Him and the power of His resurrection and the fellowship of His suffering, being conformed to His death." (Phil. 3.10). Another example is in Colossians where uses the same sort of severity and suffering entailed in sanctification, "Put to death therefore what is earthly in you: sexual immorality, impurity, passion, evil desire, and covetousness, which is idolatry" (Col. 3.5, ESV[104]). Death and suffering go hand in hand in the sanctification process and both are consequences of the cross. Because of the cross Christ suffered in the flesh, because of what the cross has effected in us, our cross bearing must also entail the afflictions which are commonly associated in our sanctification and service to Christ (cf. 2 Tim. 2.3). Luther spoke with sagacious insight on this very issue of how the cross relates to our suffering and afflictions:

> "…the cross of Christ does not mean that piece of wood that Christ carried on his shoulders and to which he was later nailed. It means generally all the afflictions of the faithful, whose sufferings

---

[104]Here the translation, "put to death" is to be preferred over the NASB "consider the members of your earthly body as dead" and draws out the imperative force of the verb ($N\varepsilon\kappa\rho\dot{\omega}\sigma\alpha\tau\varepsilon$) more lucidly.

are Christ's sufferings… There is more feeling in the head than in the other parts of the body, and Christ our Head makes all afflictions his own and suffers when we suffer, we who are his body. It is good for us to know these things, lest we should be swallowed up with sorrow or fall into despair when we see our enemies cruelly persecute, excommunicate, and kill us. But remember that we must glory in the cross, which we bear not for our own sins, but for Christ's sake."[105]

The Cross Demands Absolute Holiness

We often begin to think of sanctification and the cross as dealing mainly with conversion. The cross converts us, brings us into a right fellowship with God, it cleanses us and renews our hearts so that we no longer live unto ourselves (2 Cor. 5.15). However, we would be in error if we tend to lose sight of the cross in our daily lives, as if the cross was relevant when we initially believed, but now the cross is just a continual reminder of that day; a memorial to our conversion, nothing more. Jesus did not see His cross-work in this way. He saw the abiding significance of the cross in our daily experience and in the way we view life itself. Yet before we see how the cross consecrates us in this way, we should expose ourselves to the demands that the cross presents for each of us. Here are some of the *relevant* texts:

Matthew 10:38 [38] "And he who does not take his cross and follow after Me is not worthy of Me."

Matthew 16:24 [24] "Then Jesus said to His disciples, "If anyone wishes to come after Me, he must deny himself, and take up his cross and follow Me."

Mark 8:34 [34] "And He summoned the crowd with His disciples, and said to them, "If anyone wishes to come after Me, he must deny himself, and take up his cross and follow Me."

Luke 9:23 [23] "And He was saying to them all, "If anyone wishes to come after Me, he must deny himself, and take up his cross daily and follow Me."

---

[105]Luther, *Galatians* (1998), p.299.

Luke 14:27 [27] "Whoever does not carry his own cross and come after Me cannot be My disciple."

Without question, these texts reveal that Jesus understood taking up your cross to mean either gaining or losing life, thus the bearing of the cross was inseparable from identifying oneself with Christ through faith. Like Christ, we must make a conscience choice to "set our face towards Jerusalem" i.e. to be willing undergo suffering, to bear reproach, and to die "daily" by identifying with the cross (Lk. 9.23; cf. 1 Cor. 15.31). The cross also implies much more than God's grace to justify us *through* the cross, but also to sanctify us *with* the cross. It not only speaks of justification and definitive sanctification, it also informs our ongoing sanctification process, the progressive side of sanctification. This can be seen by the broader context of the texts above.

The Cross Consecrates

The texts above are in the context of several *disturbances* that result from our willingness and commitment to follow Christ through a cross-centered life. *First*, the cross produces consecration in the area of our earthly relationships (cf. 2 Cor. 5.16). The willingness to take up one's cross and follow Christ means that we are willing to let goods and kindred go or as Jesus says, "Follow Me, and allow the dead to bury their own dead" (Mt. 8.22). Luke ties the connection between cross-bearing and earthly relationships even closer, "If anyone comes to Me, and does not hate his own father and mother and wife and children and brothers and sisters, yes, and even his own life, he cannot be My disciple. "Whoever does not carry his own cross and come after Me cannot be My disciple." (Lk. 14.26–27).[106]

---

[106]The presence of the Present Active tense in the phrase "carry his own cross" (βαστάζει τὸν σταυρὸν ἑαυτοῦ) signifies the ongoing or continuous nature of the cross-centered life. A literal-grammatical translation of the entire verse may draw out the nuances of the Greek, "whoever is not continually and actively bearing the cross himself and continually following after Me is not able to be My disciple." Both "bearing" (βαστάζω) the cross and "coming/following" (ἔρχομαι) are present tense verbs. The pronoun is also reflexive, "*his own* cross" (τὸν σταυρὸν ἑαυτοῦ) and agrees with the Middle Voice of the verb "to come" (ἔρχομαι) and stresses the personal obligation laid upon the disciples to become identified with the cost of the cross themselves—a point which entails personal volition. See also, Garland who speaks of the "ongoing quality of living in this manner" (David E. Garland, *Luke, Exegetical Commentary on the New Testament*, vol. 3 (Grand Rapids: Zondervan, 2011) p.601).

Preaching the cross is a message about "counting the cost" (cf. Lk. 14.28ff.). It does not simply seek to present an initiation into a private spiritual life which can be adapted as one sees fit. People see Christ in almost every conceivable light yet, if not seen in the light of Scripture, sadly Jesus Christ will never rise above the fictitious picture that their human minds have contrived. People often mistake talk about having a personal relationship with Jesus to mean relating to Jesus in one's own personal way. Some view Him as a great model for wholesome living, a motivational speaker, a great holy man, or a knowledgeable man with quaint and wise sayings for all; but our subjective views of Christ are vain and meaningless without Scripture no matter how one may recast Him. Horton has wisely pointed out the utter narcissistic tendencies in our age when it comes to the priority of "the self's inner experience":

> "When push comes to shove, many Christians today justify their beliefs and practices on the basis of their own experience. Regardless of what the church teaches—or perhaps even what is taught in Scripture—the one unassailable authority in the American religion is the self's inner experience. This means, however, that it is not only one's relationship with Jesus but Jesus himself who becomes a wax figure to be molded according to whatever experiences, feelings, and felt needs one has decided to be most decisive."[107]

But in all Christian experience and human relations, *Christ* revealed in His Word is decisive, not any experience or preferences of ours. The cross means the upheaval of all previous relationships and the establishment of new ones (more on this will be said in the next chapter). It is a reordering of things where all things become new, and all regard for the most intimate and important relationships in one's life have been forever altered (Mt. 12.48-50; Jn. 19.26; 2 Cor. 5.16-17). To understand just how significantly the cross disturbs our lives, Jesus does not just call us to a different type of love; He calls us to *hate* in light of His love! Knowing our sinful tendencies, Jesus alerts us to the dangers of putting Him second to anything, even our own lives, "He who loves his life loses it, and he who hates his life in this world will keep it to life eternal" (Jn. 12.25). Ultimately the tendency within us is nothing less than the desire to subvert our Sovereign Master and erect lesser masters to serve; this is why Jesus said, "No one can serve two masters; for either he will hate the

---

[107]Horton, *Christless Christianity*, p.169-170.

one and love the other, or he will be devoted to one and despise the other. You cannot serve God and wealth" (Mt. 6.24). Jesus is pointing out the danger of having God and other things, which in the end is not to have God; He alone is to captivate our hearts to the hatred and denunciation of all else. Lloyd-Jones expounds on this fact:

> "The truth of this proposition [i.e. Mt. 6.24] is obvious. Both make a totalitarian demand upon us. Worldly things really do make a totalitarian demand as we have seen. How they tend to grip the entire personality and affect us everywhere! They demand our entire devotion; they want us to live for them absolutely. Yet, but so does God."[108]

Second, our *things* can draw us away from having cross-centered lives as well. This is why in the same context dealing with bearing our cross and counting the cost, Jesus expects us to have our priorities right concerning our possessions, "So then, none of you can be My disciple who does not give up all his own possessions" (Lk. 14.33). Like the Rich Young Ruler who would not part from the prizing of his possessions so as to prize and possess Christ for his justification, if man will not be willing to undergo the loss of "all his own possessions", again, the possibility of discipleship is lost.

Third, not only does the cross disrupt our human relationships, and every possession we may own and ever possess, the cost inherent in the cross and the cross-centered life also disrupts our personal ambitions. This too is part of true discipleship and sanctification. When Jesus called His disciples to follow Him, He often called them to surrender personal aims and personal ambitions.

Matthew 4:18–20 [18] "Now as Jesus was walking by the Sea of Galilee, He saw two brothers, Simon who was called Peter, and Andrew his brother, casting a net into the sea; for they were fishermen. [19] And He said to them, "Follow Me, and I will make you fishers of men." [20] Immediately they left their nets and followed Him."

Matthew 9:9–10 [9] "As Jesus went on from there, He saw a man called Matthew, sitting in the tax collector's booth; and He said

---

[108]Martyn Lloyd-Jones, *Studies in the Sermon the Mount*, 2nd Ed. (Grand Rapids: Eerdmans, 1976) p. 365. [Brackets mine].

to him, "Follow Me!" And he got up and followed Him. [10] Then it happened that as Jesus was reclining at the table in the house, behold, many tax collectors and sinners came and were dining with Jesus and His disciples."

Certainly, Peter, Andrew, Matthew and the others represent all others whom Jesus would call to lay down their occupations in order to follow Him. The call of the twelve was certainly unique, for they were called for a special apostolic purpose, however, the principle of discipleship holds true for all of us regardless of the sphere God may place us in for our own lives. Yet, we all have one thing in common in the cross, "And he who does not take his cross and follow after Me is not worthy of Me" (Mt. 10.38). Every true believer at some point in the Christian life must resonate with Paul's words, "I have suffered the loss of all things, and count them but rubbish so that I may gain Christ" (Phil. 3.8; cf. 1.21).

Perhaps the greatest reality of the cross is that it was not simply meant to cleanse us of our external impurities, it is not that the cross merely causes a change in hobbies and habits; it produces inner cleansing and enduring holiness as well. The author of Hebrews captures this aspect of the sanctifying power of the cross:

Hebrews 9:13-14 [13] "For if the blood of goats and bulls and the ashes of a heifer sprinkling those who have been defiled sanctify for the cleansing of the flesh, [14] how much more will the blood of Christ, who through the eternal Spirit offered Himself without blemish to God, cleanse your conscience from dead works to serve the living God?"

The glorious promise of the cross (here embodied in the code phrase, *the blood of Christ*: τὸ αἷμα τοῦ Χριστοῦ) (v.14a) is that it is sufficient to cleanse us of our previous worthless, indeed, *dead works* and to promote priestly service to the living God. The play on words in this text, *dead works* (νεκρῶν ἔργων) and *living God* (θεῷ ζῶντι) does more than simply predicate upon the attributes of God—it implies that the nature of our *works* (ἔργον) has changed, we could say, from *dead works* (νεκρῶν ἔργων) to works that are alive because we *serve the living God* (εἰς τὸ λατρεύειν θεῷ ζῶντι) who demands true spiritual service by living servants (cf. Mt. 22.32; Mk. 12.27; Lk.

20.38; Rom. 14.9).[109] After all, it was the *living God* who spoke to Moses from the fire in the midst of the burning bush and who would later call for the absolute consecration of His people (Dt. 5.26; Lev. 11.45, 19.2; 20.7).[110] As Ross points out, God's life is distinct from all other living things and gives all things their very life; this distinguishes Him from all other deities which often find their existence with counterparts in the creation itself:

> "The very first consideration of what the holiness of God means is that He is the living God, actually living, and eternally so— unlike the false gods of the pagans (who might appear to be alive) or living spirits (which were limited because they were created either by humans or God)... The Lord, then, not only created all life in order, but wants people to live according to the order of creation."[111]

Because the life of God is a holy existence He demands that His people be holy and takes it upon Himself to sanctify them, "I am the LORD who sanctifies you" (Lev. 22.32; cf. 21.8; see also, Jn. 17.17).

The cross affects us in every aspect of salvation. We are chosen in connection with the cross (Eph. 1.3-4), we are forgiven and justified through the cross (Eph. 1.7), and we are sanctified by the cross. As we live a cross-bearing, cross-centered life we become more sanctified because we become more like Christ (Gal. 2.20). But how will the cross carry us throughout life? How does the cross protect the holiness it has given to us? Does the cross fade out of sight once we have been set free by it? And how

---

[109]Romans 14.9, "For to this end Christ died and lived again, that He might be Lord both of the dead and of the living." Significant to note that even from this text we see the centrality of the cross-work of Christ (captured in the words, "Christ died" Χριστὸς ἀπέθανεν) emerge as the driving principle behind His sovereignty over "the living." Consequently, *the living* live unto God through Union with Christ (cf. Rom. 6.11).

[110]The fact that immediately following the Exodus God called His people to holiness is easily seen by the sheer number of times God commands them to be holy in the Pentateuch. Nowhere is this command found than in the book of Exodus itself where the Covenant Lord, Yahweh calls His people to take on His own holy nature by consecrating themselves as a completely distinct people marked by His holiness (e.g. Ex. 19.5-6). In Exodus alone over one hundred references and injunctions to being "holy" are found; more than any other book in Scripture.

[111]Allen P. Ross, *Holiness to the Lord, A Guide to the Exposition of the Book of Leviticus* (Grand Rapids: Baker, 2006) p.45.

do we harness the power of the cross so that it continues to have transcendent relevance in our lives, at the same time protecting us from legalism and pride? For this we must come to the text in Galatians 6.14. Here we will unpack the nature of true holiness and, sanctification, and see how the cross, not only procures that holiness, but also protects it from pride, legalism and false religion.

The Cross Protects True Holiness

In the book of Galatians Paul has sought to set out the religion of God versus the religion of man.[112] Paul has set out a worldview, in which justification by faith alone apart from human endeavor is central. This form of religion is sure to upset the Moralist, the Legalist, the Mystic, the Atheist, the Agnostic, and the Post-Modern. For Paul, true religion is the religion of God's free grace, it is the gospel of Jesus Christ who saves His people from their sins on the basis of grace through the agency of faith alone apart from human merit (Eph. 2.8-10). This is what sets men right with God (Gal. 2.15-16). Therefore, the gospel is not of human origin neither is it a self-help program, the gospel is not civility or religiosity, it is a religion *extra nos* (outside of us) which has come down to us through a supernatural revelation and a supernatural incarnation (Lk. 2.8ff.). Salvation is a plan (Eph. 3.8-11). Salvation is a decree that originates in the eternal counsels of God's mind (Hab. 1.5; Acts 13.41). It is the design of the Creator God to work all things after His own inscrutable counsel, for the purpose of upholding His eternal and undiminishable glory, through the redemption of a people chosen and given to the Son by the Father, who commune by the Spirit in everlasting triune joy (Jn. 17.5).

The cross comes in as the emblem of all of this salvation. As Calvin noted, "In the cross redemption in all its parts is found."[113] The grandeur of salvation by grace through faith has been embossed by the cross, the

---

[112]What Paul identifies as, "the elemental things of the world" ($τὰ \ στοιχεῖα \ τοῦ \ κόσμου$) and "the weak and worthless elemental things" ($τὰ \ ἀσθενῆ \ καὶ \ πτωχὰ \ στοιχεῖα$); see also (Col. 2.8, 20). It seems from the context of Paul's usage, the term "elemental" ($στοιχεῖον$) is to be taken as man's basic worldview principles or teachings which are devoid of Christ. In this sense the term can refer either to Jewish or Gentile teachings which are contrary to the gospel and as Bruce suggests "belonged to a pre-Christian stage of experience" which "to accept it now would be a mark of spiritual retrogression" (see, F.F. Bruce, *The Epistles to the Colossians, to Philemon, and to the Ephesians, New International Commentary on the New Testament* (Grand Rapids: Eerdmans, 1984) p. 100).

[113]John Calvin, *Calvin's Commentaries* (Grand Rapids: Baker, 2005) vol. XXI, p.184.

imprint of God's love upon the hearts of those who are being saved by God's power (Rom. 1.16; 5.5). In Galatians 6.14, the apostle Paul makes his final comparison between those of the circumcision or better, "the mutilation" (cf. Phil. 3.2), and his own faithful ministry. With this verse Paul not only gives us several marks of his ministry but he also supplies us with various aspects of the cross' sanctifying power. Again, as we will see below, the cross-centered life prohibits pride, prohibits legalism, and promotes true religion or holiness. Paul says:

Galatians 6:14 [14] "But may it never be that I would boast, except in the cross of our Lord Jesus Christ, through which the world has been crucified to me, and I to the world."

The Cross Prohibits Pride

When boasting does not have as its object the cross itself, it becomes worthless pride. However, when the cross is the object of our boasting, pride is replaced with godly humility. When Paul refused to boast in anything other than the cross, he included himself. Paul did not boast in what he had achieved, unless of course it was for the sake of showing his opponents the logical absurdity of their own pride (cf. 2 Cor. 7.4; 11.21ff.; 12.1-6; Phil. 3.2-6). In every chapter of Paul's life and ministry, the cross had so humbled Paul that his ministry was done in the meekness of Christ and empowered solely by the Spirit of Christ (1 Cor. 2.4-5). Even in adverse situations Paul remained in a humble frame of heart. Whether in the midst of disciplinary issues in the church (2 Cor. 10.1) or in the context of persecution, Paul maintained a cross-centered ministry through exemplary, humble service to Christ and His church:

Acts 20:17-19 [17] "From Miletus he sent to Ephesus and called to him the elders of the church. [18] And when they had come to him, he said to them, "You yourselves know, from the first day that I set foot in Asia, how I was with you the whole time, [19] serving the Lord with all humility and with tears and with trials which came upon me through the plots of the Jews.""

It was through the cross that Paul's religious zeal and blood lust was brought to an end, that is, "when God… was pleased to reveal His Son" to Paul on the Damascus Road calling him instead to suffer for the name he once hated, the name of Jesus of Nazareth (Gal. 1.15-16; Acts 9.1-

16). This is how the cross overcomes our pride; it replaces our pride with deepest humility. As Piper rightly pointed out; *the cross* overcomes God's resistance to our pride as well as overcoming our pride against God:

> "In the cross of Christ, God has undertaken to overcome both obstacles to preaching. It overcomes the objective, external obstacle of God's righteous opposition to human pride. And it overcomes the subjective, internal obstacle of our proud opposition to God's glory. In so doing the cross becomes the ground of the objective validity of preaching and the ground of the subjective humility of preaching."[114]

Paul's humility should not be seen merely as referring to his visible demeanor, it should not be seen as simply a tone in his voice, mannerisms and gestures, facial expressions, or anything of the like. More than an attitude or a characteristic in the person of Paul, the humility of Paul was a mindset rooted in the cross (cf. Phil. 2.1-5). It was a cross-centered world and life view which informed his personal life and his preaching. Piper goes on to give further comments on the nature of how the cross affects our preaching by prohibiting pride:

> "The cross is also the ground of the humility of preaching because the cross is the power of God to crucify the pride of both preacher and congregation. In the New Testament the cross is not only a past place of objective substitution; it is also a present place of subjective execution—the execution of my self-reliance and my love affair with the praise of man. "Far be it from me to boast except in the cross of our Lord Jesus Christ, by which the world has been crucified to me, and I to the world (Gal. 6:14)."[115]

The mercy that Paul had been shown was immense (cf. 2 Cor. 4.1). He had been forgiven of his sins, he had been forgiven for fighting against God and his people (Acts 26.14), and he had been forgiven for being an ignorant enemy of God and for causing Christians to utter blasphemies against God's Holy Servant, Jesus (Acts 26.11). But the gospel made Paul loathe himself and cast off any notion of self-reliance, depending solely

---

[114]John Piper, *The Supremacy of God in Preaching* (Grand Rapids: Baker, 2004) p.33.
[115]Ibid. p.36-37.

on the sovereign mercy of God (Phil. 3.7; 1 Tim. 1.12-16). Paul wanted to communicate something of this humbling understanding to the churches, that they too may come to see their lives in a more Christ-centered way and thus, in a more cross-centered way. The Corinthians who lived in a culture much like our own today, one that prided itself on its wisdom, education, fashion, culture, athletic abilities, and personal achievements, needed desperately to have their pride stripped from them through the cross:

> **1 Corinthians 1:25–31** 25 "Because the foolishness of God is wiser than men, and the weakness of God is stronger than men. 26 For consider your calling, brethren, that there were not many wise according to the flesh, not many mighty, not many noble; 27 but God has chosen the foolish things of the world to shame the wise, and God has chosen the weak things of the world to shame the things which are strong, 28 and the base things of the world and the despised God has chosen, the things that are not, so that He may nullify the things that are, 29 so that no man may boast before God. 30 But by His doing you are in Christ Jesus, who became to us wisdom from God, and righteousness and sanctification, and redemption, 31 so that, just as it is written, "Let him who boasts, boast in the Lord."

I think he places a particular emphasis on v.30, "by His doing you are in Christ Jesus". It is only through the preaching of the cross, which can humble both preacher and congregation. It reminds us, as Paul does here, that we were once foolish, weak, unwise, lacking might, lacking nobility, foolish things, the weak things of the world, base things, despised, "things that are not", in other words, we were nothing! Whatever our own sinful wisdom once said that we were the wisdom of the cross has smashed it to pieces, in order to show us that we are nothing without God's saving activity in our lives.

It is not until a person is "in Christ Jesus" that he/she partakes of God's wisdom, righteousness, sanctification, and redemption. For this reason no one can commend themselves to God. No one can say, "I am circumcised", "I keep the Sabbath", "I am a pretty good, moral, considerate, law-abiding person". No one can commend themselves before God through personal achievement and religiously generated righteousness (cf. Jer. 9.23-24; Gal. 2.16; Phil. 3.9-11; Tit. 3.5).

The Cross Prohibits Legalism

As we look further to the book of Galatians for Paul's cross-centered theology, we should bear in mind what Galatians consists of. The letter to the Galatians is a constant testimony of the non-negotiable nature of the gospel of free grace where the righteousness of God is conferred on sinners *by faith*. The gospel is the summary of the plan of redemption where God has chosen to save a people from their sins in order that they might live to the praise of *His* glory (Eph. 1.6, 12, 14). The cross of Jesus Christ is the zenith, the apex, summit and soul of the gospel. It is the intersection between God's saving grace and man's sinful misery. The cross is the very kernel of God's saving purpose. The cross is the most precious, least expendable, greatest display of the love of God the world has ever known (Jn. 3.16; 15.13; Rom. 3.25; 5.6-8; Eph. 5.2; 1 Jn. 4.9-11). Beneath the weight of that, those who are effectually drawn by the grace of God to Jesus Christ, simultaneously have their minds illuminated to the glory of the cross and the misery of their sin. This is what Galatians seeks to highlight by removing human merit as the *basis* of one's right standing before God (Gal. 2.16). Once man's works have been removed from the equation of justification, we are left gazing solely upon the cross-work of Christ. The humility of the gospel Paul preached was rooted in the pride-destroying, all-sufficient cross-work of Jesus Christ.

This is why Paul can say, "But may it never be that I would boast, except in the cross of our Lord Jesus Christ" (Gal. 6.14a). Legalism always leads to improper boasting. But the cross destroys legalism both for those who are justified and for those who teach the gospel of justification. Paul stresses that the Judaizers want to have boasting surround their religious zeal, their effectiveness in producing converts, and their devotion to Jewish custom through circumcision:

> **Galatians 6:13** [13] "For those who are circumcised do not even keep the Law themselves, but they desire to have you circumcised so that they may boast in your flesh."

Boasting in their convert's *flesh* was a sure sign of legalism, since it meant that they lauded their ability to bring others into external conformity to the Law even though, as is the case with all legalism, the Judaizers "do not even keep the Law themselves." Because only the cross could justify, Paul could not boast in anything else "except in the cross" (εἰ μὴ ἐν τῷ σψαυρῷ). In this way the cross prohibits pride and ensures humility to the glory of God.

The Cross Promotes True Religion

Neither legalism nor spiritual pride can promote true religion, true spirituality, or true holiness in God's people. Indeed, scores of Christian literature has emerged in recent years to show us how to be sanctified. Some stressing that we cannot be sanctified without certain methodologies of prayer or certain types of musings in our private journals, or that unless we go through certain courses by the latest popular author and purchase the corresponding literature we cannot be truly spiritual. For Paul, however, only the work of the cross is great enough to sanctify us and render us dead to the world, dead to sin and dead to false notions of spirituality. For Paul, the cross was antithetical to the *world*.[116] Luther's classic commentary on Galatians is helpful to see the antithesis:

"Paul regards the world as damned, and the world regards him as damned. He abhors all the doctrine, righteousness, and acts of the world as the poison of the devil. The world detests Paul's doctrine and acts and regards him as a seditious, pernicious, pestilent fellow and a heretic. The world's judgment concerning religion and righteousness before God is contrary to the judgment of godly people, because God and the devil are contrary to one another. God is crucified to the devil, and the devil to God; God condemns the doctrine and acts of the devil (1 Jn. 3:8), and the devil condemns and overthrows the Word and acts of God, for he is a murderer and the father of lies. So the world condemns the doctrine of the life of godly people, calling them pernicious heretics and troublers of the public peace. And faithful people call the world the son of the devil, following its father's steps as a murderer and liar... Thus Paul shows that he hates the world with the perfect hatred of the Holy Spirit; and the world hates him with the total hatred of a wicked spirit."[117]

---

[116]Here the word, "world" (κόσμος), refers not to creation, the universe, or humanity as such; instead "world" refers to "the present evil age" (τοῦ αἰῶαος τοῦ ἐνεστῶτος πονηροῦ) of Pauline thought elsewhere (Gal. 1.4). For Paul the *world* was the world system comprised of sin, false teaching, and satanic influence which lead people away from Christ and the gospel rather than to it (cf. 1Cor. 1.20ff.; 2 Cor. 4.4; Eph. 2.1).

[117]Luther, *Galatians*, p.300.

As we have seen, the cross' power to sanctify is seen in the humility that it creates in us by stripping us of self-righteousness. Pure religion produces the right type of *sacrifice* and the right type of satisfaction. *Religion* can be a good or bad word depending on how it is used. Here the term operates in harmony with James' timeless words, "Pure and undefiled religion in the sight of our God and Father is this: to visit orphans and widows in their distress, and to keep oneself unstained by the world" (Jam. 1:27). Properly understood then, *pure religion* is undefiled when it produces a truly sacrificial life of good deeds. It also means that God is so sanctifying us that the present evil age does not defile us with its sensual pleasures so that we fall out of love with the world and in love with God (cf. 1 Jn. 2.15-17). This is precisely what the cross produced in Paul, the right type of sacrifice through his service to Christ and the right type of satisfaction through his devotion and love for Christ. For Paul, the cross rendered him dead to world and the world dead to him. For Paul, like Luther after him, the world (properly understood) was "the son of the devil" because of its opposition to Christ and its commitment to the evil one.

Galatians 6.14 is Paul's exclamation point in his argument to the Galatians because it kills self-righteousness through the cross. This text also captures the essence of this dual aspect of true spirituality, namely the death of Paul and the death of the world around him. When Paul says that it was "through" (δἰ) the cross that "the world has been crucified to me, and I to the world" (ἐμοὶ κόσηος ἐσταύρωται κἀγὼ κόσμω);[118] he means to say that the cross resulted in a life orientation of humility and holiness that redefined who he was and how he lived. Paul's expression is perfectly balanced. The expression has two parts which work towards the same overall picture he is trying to give, namely that two things have died through crucifixion i.e. the world and himself. We should look at both of these realities closer to better understand Paul's theology of the cross and how it effects sanctification.

First, in pointing out the relevance of the cross for Christian theology and the Christian life; the apostles after Christ came to see the deeper significances of the cross—that ancient symbol of cruelty. Thus statements

---

[118]Paul's word order here may reflect an intended emphasis. By putting the emphatic (ἐμοὶ) at the head of the clause he may wish to stress the fact that it is *his* orientation in this life that has changed not the world's. This fits well with Pauline theology elsewhere (cf. Rom. 12.2; 1 Cor. 1.18; 3.19).

about the cross only have theological relevance because of Christ. It is the cross of "our Lord Jesus Christ", not just any cross. In the ancient world crucifixion was taboo talk. Jesus transformed an otherwise obscene symbol into a symbol of pure holiness. What was only associated with death now came to represent life; once an ancient symbol of humiliation and social curse (and for Jews divine curse cf. Dt. 21.23) came to speak of honor and blessing. Thus, the cross becomes the instrument through which the believer dies to the world and the world dies to the believer. As Dietrich Bonhoeffer once put it, "it is a death full of grace."[119] As Ferguson has pointed out, the cross is an inverted symbol which is now God's "instrument of reconciliation" and "symbol of forgiveness":

> "When Paul preached "the cross" he preached a message which explained that this instrument of rejection had been used by God as His instrument of reconciliation. Man's means of bringing death to Jesus was God's means to bring life to the world. Man's symbol of rejecting Christ was God's symbol of forgiveness for man. This is why Paul boasted about the cross!"[120]

Not only did Christ through His death change the significance of the cross, the cross changed the relationship of the world to His people (cf. Jn. 7.7). Paul insists that the world has taken on a certain *deadness* through the cross. Just as the *aliveness* of the world cannot be understood apart from Paul's own life in the world (i.e. apart from Christ), so too, the deadness of the world cannot be separated from Paul's death through this metaphorical crucifixion. It is precisely because the apostle is *dead* that the world has lost its own *soul* so far as he is concerned. Because the world has been *crucified*, it no longer has any power to distinguish Paul, to define him, and capture his ultimate allegiance. Although he has no confusion about abiding in the world as earthly citizen, his ultimate citizenship is in heaven (Phil. 3.20). Paul's identity is no longer marked out by this world of sin and misery, he has a new cross-centered identity. Paul has been chosen out of the world and is therefore now hated by the world since he is no longer of the world as Jesus Himself was not *of the world*. Like Israel of old, believers undergo their own personal consecration through the cross. What Jesus told the disciples was inevitably true of Paul, "I have given them Your word; and the world has hated them,

---

[119]Dietrich Bonhoeffer, The Cost of Discipleship (New York: Macmillan, 1968) pp. 258.

[120]Sinclair B. Ferguson, Grow in Grace, (Carlisle, PA: Banner of Truth Trust, 1989) p. 55.

because they are not of the world, even as I am not of the world" (Jn. 17.14). For Paul, the old order of things had been shattered by the cross (2 Cor. 5.17)—a reality of which he reminded the Ephesians:

Ephesians 2:1–7 [1] "And you were dead in your trespasses and sins, [2] in which you formerly walked according to the course of this world, according to the prince of the power of the air, of the spirit that is now working in the sons of disobedience. [3] Among them we too all formerly lived in the lusts of our flesh, indulging the desires of the flesh and of the mind, and were by nature children of wrath, even as the rest. [4] But God, being rich in mercy, because of His great love with which He loved us, [5] even when we were dead in our transgressions, made us alive together with Christ (by grace you have been saved), [6] and raised us up with Him, and seated us with Him in the heavenly places in Christ Jesus, [7] so that in the ages to come He might show the surpassing riches of His grace in kindness toward us in Christ Jesus."

The *second* aspect of Paul's statement focuses on Paul's relationship to the world. He too has been put to death through crucifixion so that he no longer has a relationship to the world as once he did. This means of course that Paul is focusing on the fact that he has undergone a radical transformation himself resulting in a severed relationship with the world (properly defined). He is undergoing sanctification whereby he is putting to death the deeds of the body. He is no longer enslaved to the lusts of the world which once trapped him in the prison of self-righteousness. Although Paul may have lived what looked like a good, moral and, indeed, religious life in Judaism, nevertheless his zeal was rooted in the ignorance of justification by faith alone through Christ alone without whom he would also be consigned under sin (Rom. 3.9). As Paul mentions in many other places, he has died with Christ and the only life (identity) he knows now is that which is "hidden with Christ":

Romans 6:1–4 [1] "What shall we say then? Are we to continue in sin so that grace may increase? [2] May it never be! How shall we who died to sin still live in it? [3] Or do you not know that all of us who have been baptized into Christ Jesus have been baptized into His death? [4] Therefore we have been buried with Him through baptism into death, so that as Christ was raised from the dead through the glory of the Father, so we too might walk in newness of life."

Galatians 2:20 [20] "I have been crucified with Christ; and it is no longer I who live, but Christ lives in me; and the life which I now live in the flesh I live by faith in the Son of God, who loved me and gave Himself up for me."

Colossians 3:3–4 [3] "For you have died and your life is hidden with Christ in God. [4] When Christ, who is our life, is revealed, then you also will be revealed with Him in glory."[121]

Too often the cross is presented with cheap grace, little or no obedience, and seemingly very little expectations placed upon the lives of the converted.[122] However, for Paul, everything was different once he encountered the cross. He had forsaken his former ways in Judaism (Gal. 1.13-15), he had left behind whatever selfish ambitions he once had, as did the rest of the apostles (cf. Mt. 19.27), he had lost sight of his religious and ethnic pedigree in order to obtain true righteousness and life in Christ (Phil. 3.4-8). Furthermore, this life altering transformation of the cross never wore off for Paul. Paul never seemed to have receded in his pursuit of Christ. His passion to know Him remained steadfast until the end. Paul never drew back from the cross, he never ran back to the fleeting pleasures of sin or the lusts which the world had to offer him. Paul's trajectory was always God-ward, a trajectory set in motion through the cross (cf. 1 Pet. 3.18).

The remarkable thing about the text of Galatians 6.14 is not the *death* of the world, nor even that of Paul, but what has caused these two simultaneous *crucifixions* in the first place. The context is clear that it was *the cross* that caused the sanctification we have looked at here, where both Paul and the world have been rendered simultaneously dead to each other.[123] This is why Paul glories in *the cross* and not in something else. It is important to remember that Paul was not simply acknowledging the work of the cross along merely doctrinal lines, but indeed he boasted in

---

[121]In the context of this passage we should notice how naturally one's union with Christ i.e. identifying with His life and death leads to sanctification (Col. 3.5ff.). On this theme see also, Rom. 6.1-6; 2 Cor. 5.17; Eph. 2.4-10).

[122]See especially, John MacArthur, *The Gospel According to Jesus* (Grand Rapids: Zondervan, 2011).

[123]Exegetically we should point out that the voice of the Greek verb "to crucify" (σταυρόω) is passive and it refers back to "the cross" (τῷ σταυρῷ) in (Gal. 6.14a) as the causal factor for both the crucifixion of the world to Paul (ἐμοὶ κόσμος ἐσταύρωται) and Paul to the world (κἀγὼ κόσμῳ).

the cross, he gloried in the cross because he treasured the cross in the affections of his heart as well. As Calvin points out, "Where man's highest good exists, there is his glory".[124] Schreiner captures the implications of the cross-centered boasting of Paul here:

> "The cross of Jesus Christ has introduced the new creation (6:15). The present evil age no longer rules over those who have been delivered by the cross. Those who boast in the cross understand that the law does not bring righteousness; the cross kills the old person and introduces a new reality (2:21). The curse of the law has been removed by Christ's taking the curse on Himself (3:13), and hence those who boast in the cross rejoice in their deliverance from the elements of the world and their freedom from the law (4:3–5)."[125]

This notion of glorying in the cross is crucial when talking about true spirituality against legalism on the one side and Antinomianism on the other. When we glory in the power of the cross, we cannot glory in ourselves. We are forced to steer away from Moralism because the separation that has emerged between us and the present evil age is not of our doing (cf. 1 Cor. 1.30). We have been taken out of the world and united *to* Christ *by* Christ and *for* Christ. Solely by identifying with the death and life of Christ empowered and led by His Spirit (Gal. 5.16-17; Phil. 3.9-11) will we live lives separated to God for holiness.

Also when we boast only in the cross, we will treasure it above all sin and all sinful pleasures and above all that the world has to offer us. Paul did not simply say, "may I never forget to boast in the cross among other things" or "may I always remember to boast also in the cross"; he said, "may it never be that I would boast *except* in the cross." Not simply because the cross is that which justifies, but in addition to that and flowing from that, the cross also sanctifies and sets us apart to live lives of holiness for the sake of the One who died in our place. Preaching the cross is preaching Christ.

Thus, to preach Christ crucified is to preach *the cost of discipleship*, to call sinners to a holy life; a cruciform life where the *cross* always shapes

---

[124]John Calvin, *Calvin's Commentaries*, p.184.

[125]Thomas R. Schreiner, *Galatians, Zondervan Exegetical Commentary on the New Testament* (Grand Rapids, MI: Zondervan, 2010), p.379.

our hearts and lives. The cross is what sets our sanctification in motion and makes us like Christ. The reason we ought to plead with people about the holy demands of the cross is because the cross is an invitation to die, that is, to live no longer for oneself but for the One who died for them (2 Cor. 5.15). The cross casts a shadow of profound demands over our lives as it bids us to come and die (Lk. 14.27). The cross means the end of life as we once knew it (2 Cor. 5.16) and, relationships as we once knew them, even our closest familial bonds are often cut asunder by the life shattering power of the cross (Mt. 12.48-50). The cross is also a daily struggle because sanctification is daily. To bear your cross is to suffer. When Jesus called people to follow Him, He called them under the guise of associating with His death; indeed His curse absorbing cross:

> **Philippians 3:7–11** [7] "But whatever things were gain to me, those things I have counted as loss for the sake of Christ. [8] More than that, I count all things to be loss in view of the surpassing value of knowing Christ Jesus my Lord, for whom I have suffered the loss of all things, and count them but rubbish so that I may gain Christ, [9] and may be found in Him, not having a righteousness of my own derived from the Law, but that which is through faith in Christ, the righteousness which comes from God on the basis of faith, [10] that I may know Him and the power of His resurrection and the fellowship of is sufferings, being conformed to His death; [11] in order that I may attain to the resurrection from the dead."

The cross gave Paul both an eschatological view of life and a proper eternal perspective of the triviality of things in comparison to knowing the crucified Jesus.

For this reason, the cross can be understood to consecrate us in every facet of life—relationships, occupations, and even our possessions are laid down at the foot of the cross as part of the weight of our discipleship. To be identified with the cross is to be cleansed by the cross. After all it was at the cross where Jesus sheds His precious blood, makes perfect atonement for His people, and redeems us for His holy purposes (Phil. 1.19-20). The cross is how God cleanses us from dead works and sets us apart to be His living servants (Heb. 9.14). Like Paul we must be resolved never to lose sight of the cross. We are called to live a cross-centered life and to boast only in the cross throughout all of life (Gal. 6.14). As we look back to the cross we see God's merciful logo of the merits of Christ. The cross represents all of our salvation; justification, reconciliation, propitiation and it secures true spirituality with God. Because the cross has rendered us dead to the world and alive to Christ, we cannot boast in anything except the cross and we cannot live by any other creed aside from the cross.[126] The cross strips us of our Christ-belittling pride, self-exalting legalism, and promotes ongoing holiness in the power of the Spirit. The beauty of the gospel of Christ crucified is that it has transformed that ancient symbol of fallen cruelty into an emblem of everlasting righteousness, and in doing so it bestows divine blessing instead of divine curse and opens the way to eternal life.

---

[126]When NT authors often speak of the cross they are referring not simply to the physical object, the historical event of the crucifixion, or even the death of Christ. Certainly these are assumed but the "cross" (σταυρός) becomes *code* for the redemptive work of Jesus Christ—the crosswork of Jesus.

6

CRUCIFIED TO GATHER US,
PREACHING THE CORPORATE
DIMENSIONS OF THE CROSS

Few things seem to be more controversial today in the teachings of Scripture than *Ecclesiology*. One's theology of the Church can often manifest the authenticity of a person's commitment to Christ. With the rise of seeker sensitivity, consumer-driven methods of ministry, technological integration and multi-site models for *doing church*, personal participation and biblical church membership has taken on new challenges. In his recent treatment of church membership and discipline, Jonathan Leeman defines church membership as follows:

> "Church membership is (1) a covenant of union between a particular church and a Christian, a covenant that consists of (2) the church's affirmation of the Christian's gospel profession, (3) the church's promise to give oversight to the Christian, and (4) the Christian's promise to gather with the church and submit to its oversight."[127]

Sadly, even today many are abandoning even this basic formula for what membership is. As the modern church seeks to *keep up with the times* too often our Scripture based focus for church gives way to more extra-biblical ways of doing ministry. But extra-biblical and finally, unbiblical concepts of church result in undermining one aspect of the cross-work of Christ, which is so vital to the gospel—*the fact that Christ died for the church He instituted with His blood and instructs with His word.* The corporate dimensions of the cross therefore have to be revisited, reaffirmed and reasserted

---

[127]Jonathan Leeman, *The Church and the Surprising Offense of God's Love, Reintroducing the Doctrines of Church Membership and Discipline* (Wheaton, IL: Crossway, 2010) p.217.

as essential to true Christian experience—essential to what the gospel is all about. It does no good to dilute Scripture's teaching of ecclesiology, since that would only lead to weakening the power and effectiveness of the church in a postmodern, post-Christian culture. The church is often persuaded under the pressures of political correctness to abandon unpopular teachings of Scripture like church membership, church discipline, and biblical complementarian church leadership, etc. Ironically, it is the unbelieving world that often takes notice when God's people begin to shy away from declaring the whole counsel of God. One recent headline in mainstream media comes to mind.

CNN editor, Steven James, recently wrote an article which made the "front page" of CNN.com. The article was entitled, *Stop sugar coating the Bible*. In the article, James proceeded to chide Christians for essentially watering down the Biblical text by hiding things, like Scripture's use of real life situations and harsh language. Steven expressed a number of frustrations:

> "God's message was not meant to be run through some arbitrary, holier-than-thou politeness filter. He [God] intended the Bible to speak to people where they're at, caught up in the stark reality of life on a fractured planet. And rather than shy away from difficult and painful topics, the Old Testament includes vivid descriptions of murder, cannibalism, witchcraft, dismemberment, torture, rape, idolatry, erotic sex and animal sacrifice. According to St. Paul, those stories were written as examples and warnings for us (1 Corinthians 10:11). So obviously they were meant to be retold without editing out all the things we don't consider nice or agreeable."[128]

I pray that when James says, "those stories were written as examples and warnings for *us*", he was referring to the fact that *he* has personally trusted in Christ alone for salvation. James ends the article with the words, "We don't need to edit God." What a lamentable reality it is when the secular news reels need to confront the Church with the raw truth of the Word of God. Regardless of James' faith, what he pointed out reveals what I believe to be a systemic problem in the church today (i.e. the

[128]http://religion.blogs.cnn.com/2012/02/25/my-take-stop-sugarcoating-the-bible/?hpt=hp_c1. [brackets mine].

unwillingness of the Church to simply stand up and tell the truth about what Scripture really teaches regarding the types of things which Steven James mentions), yes, but even more so the things which pertain to the central message of Scripture itself in the gospel. The truth that salvation is through no other name than Jesus Christ, and through no other means than the cross of Christ, in order to gather to Himself a new humanity in Christ and all to the exclusive glory of God. Unlike many in the Church today, Paul did not need the world to remind him of the raw truths of Scripture. He did not need anyone to inform him about the controversy surrounding the teachings of Scripture on anything; not least of which is the controversial nature of church membership.

To use James' words above, Ecclesiology tends to make Christians *edit God*. The purpose of the cross, however, will not allow for this emendation to Christian theology. To diminish the corporate dimensions of the cross is a major loss. Many people today claim they want nothing to do with Christ precisely because of some *experience* (usually negative) in the church. People complain about the hypocrisy of the church, the greed of the church, the materialistic focus of the church, especially with regards to expensive capital campaigns and building projects, and the list goes on and on. There can be no question that some have been hurt by the church, let down by the church, and offended by gross hypocrisy in the church, yet that is no reason to abandon Scripture's teaching on what the church is and why the church exists. The truth is that there's an inseparable relationship that exists between a person's participation in the visible and local church and their introduction spiritually into the invisible, universal Church. Furthermore, this chapter will focus on how the cross-work of Christ informs all of this and what God is doing, through salvation, to gather His people into a corporate entity called the Church. We also have to consider the cross-centered nature of the life of the local church and why Paul's preaching of Christ crucified cannot be understood apart from this ecclesiastical focus.

If, as we noted in chapter five, the cross is God's emblem of His everlasting love toward us, whereby He saves and sanctifies us, how are we going to remember that and set Christ's cross-work ever before us in the church? How are we going to continue to be ever mindful of the cross and focused on the cross in the church? After all, the songs, worship, and liturgy of many churches gives occasion for the church to sing about the cross, praise God for the cross and evoke the cross as the beacon of salvation, but remarkably, and in a real way, it seems many today still forget the centrality of the cross. How will the church bring that centrality back to the forefront? In a very gracious way, God has done that for us. It is built into the very DNA of the church itself if we understand what the church is and how it ought to operate. The church being purchased by God's blood (Acts 20.28) has also been given Christ's cross-centered traits as the foundations of the church (cf. 1 Tim. 3.14-16). This was a very gracious thing in that God did not leave it up to His church to think of ways to remember the cross; He gives us these ways by the very way in which He designed the church to function. Virtually every aspect of the church can somehow be concentrically connected back to the cross. Theologically speaking, all of Scripture pivots on the cross in both a *centrifugal* and *centripetal* fashion. All things point *to* the cross and away *from* the cross. Scripture moves towards the center of the cross in a centrifugal fashion with great expectation and Scripture also moves out from the center of the cross centripetally with great theological implications in practically every area of Christian thought. In a real sense, the cross is a *fulcrum* cross, Christ a fulcrum Savior upon which all of redemption hinges and turns.

In the Shadow of the Cross

Because much of the focus here is spent on New Covenant life and how God orients our worship and ministry around the cross, we should briefly appreciate how God pointed His Old Covenant people forward to the cross in expectation and anticipation of its salvific work.

From the very beginning of God's saving purposes, the cross has been in God's mind. With respect to the gospel and the riches of what he called "the administration of the mystery"[129] Paul said, "this was in accordance with the eternal purpose which He carried out in Christ Jesus our Lord" (Eph. 3.11). For this reason the whole scheme of redemption is eternally cross-centered.[130] This cross-centeredness, then, does not begin with the book of Acts or even the Gospels; in a very real and prophetic

---

[129]Gk. ἡ οἰκονομία τοῦ μυστηρίου.

[130]For another passage which draws out God's eternal purpose to save His people through the crosswork of Christ from all eternity see: Rev.13.8. There the Revelator implies that God's people are those whose names are written in The Book of Life which belongs to and is associated with "the Lamb who was slain."

sense, the cross has been anticipated since the opening chapters of the Bible. In fact, to read Scripture without this anticipatory note is to read Scripture *a*—Christologically i.e. without Christ and therefore without the key to Scripture itself (cf. Lk. 24.25-26, 44-46). It does no good to read about creation, the image of God in man, the great flood, the patriarchal promises, the Exodus, the giving of the Law, the institutions of Israel, the building and rebuilding of the temple, the promise of land and rest, the captivities, the exiles, and the promise of future restoration for the people of God without reading Scripture in a cross-centered way.[131] We will briefly visit this Christ-centered anticipatory theme before moving on to the cross-centered nature of the New Testament church.

Paul taught that Jesus is the second and last Adam (1 Cor. 15.45). He is the federal/covenant head of all His people just as Adam was the representative of his people (cf. Rom. 5.12ff.). He represents us *again* before God and earns the righteousness that Adam could not gain. However, lest we should think that Jesus is a mere parallel to the first Adam, we should be careful to note what kind of Adam Jesus was—a vastly *superior* Adam to the first. Rather than being confronted with temptation, Jesus was thrust or *impelled*[132] into temptation by the Spirit (Mk. 1.12). Furthermore, Jesus unlike Adam was not tempted in such a kind environment as that found in Eden. Mark is careful to note that Jesus was tempted among "the wild beasts" (Mk. 1.13). This is vastly different than the conditions of the Garden where Adam and Eve had dominion over the beasts which at the time were vegetarian and subdued under man's

---

[131]It is beyond the scope of the present volume to delve into the theme of Christ in the OT; however several excellent works have been produced on the subject: Edmund P. Clowney, *The Unfolding Mystery* (Philipsburg: P & R, 1988); Clowney, *Preaching Christ in all of Scripture* (Wheaton: Crossway, 2003); Dennis E. Johnson, *Him We Proclaim, Preaching Christ from all the Scriptures* (Philipsburg: P&R, 2007); G.K. Beale & D.A. Carson, *Commentary on the New Testament Use of the Old* (Grand Rapids: Baker, 2007); Peter J. Gentry & Stephen J. Wellum, *Kingdom through Covenant, A Biblical-Theological Understanding of the Covenants* (Wheaton: Crossway, 2012); O. Palmer Robertson, *The Christ of the Covenants* (Philipsburg: P&R, 1980); *The Christ of the Prophets* (Philipsburg: P&R, 2004); Christopher J.H. Wright, *Knowing Jesus through the Old Testament* (Downers-Grove: IVP, 1995). Although I would differ at various points with the aforementioned authors, their work is nevertheless of great value for seeing the prominent place Christ holds in all of Scripture.

[132]Mark's word is unique among the other temptation accounts. The Greek word (ἐκβάλλω) literally means Jesus was forcefully driven out. Instead of seeking to avoid temptation, Jesus in the power of the Spirit, put Himself in the direct path of temptation, and that seemingly by an undisguised Devil.

sovereignty. His temptation was much more severe, also, in the fact that He was tempted for forty days and forty nights[133] (Mk. 1.13; Mt. 4.2; Lk. 4.2), and tempted under a weaker human condition being physically deprived of food and water (Mt. 4.2; Lk. 4.2), not to mention that Jesus was being tempted with objects of greater seduction: food when He was hungry (Lk. 4.3), the chance to rule over the world which would soon rise up to kill Him (Lk. 4.5-6), and premature death whereby He could escape the horrors of the cross (Lk. 4.9). In all these things Jesus succeeds where Adam failed. But finally, it was through the death of the second Adam that He would become "a life giving spirit" (1 Cor. 15.45). Jesus is God's true Son; one with whom God is pleased (Mt. 17.5). For this reason Jesus is said to be God's very image (2 Cor. 4.4). He is not simply an image bearer, created in the image God (for He was not created at all), but actually was the full expression of God's image:

> **2 Corinthians 4:3–4** [3] "And even if our gospel is veiled, it is veiled to those who are perishing, [4] in whose case the god of this world has blinded the minds of the unbelieving so that they might not see the light of the gospel of the glory of Christ, who is the image of God."

> **Colossians 1:15** [15] "He is the image of the invisible God, the firstborn of all creation."

> **Hebrews 1:1–3** [1] "God, after He spoke long ago to the fathers in the prophets in many portions and in many ways, [2] in these last days has spoken to us in His Son, whom He appointed heir of all things, through whom also He made the world. [3] And He is the radiance of His glory and the exact representation of His nature, and upholds all things by the word of His power. When He had made purification of sins, He sat down at the right hand of the Majesty on high…"

Jesus could tell His disciples that if they had seen Him they had, in essence, seen the Father, since Jesus as the image of God is the exact representation of the Father (Jn. 14.9). Jesus was God's image, and thus

---

[133]Forty days and forty night being another significant redemptive number pregnant with Old Testament meaning and imagery. Old Testament imagery is so magnificently layered over the person and work of Christ the details would take the present volume in a totally different direction.

an exact representation of His nature, perfectly reflecting and representing the deepest part of God, His glory, "For God, who said, "Light shall shine out of darkness," is the One who has shone in our hearts to give the Light of the knowledge of the glory of God in the face of Christ" (2 Cor. 4.6). God created man in His image *because* of Jesus Christ. Reflecting on, "the Son, who is the Father's exact representation" Anthony Hoekema explains the purpose of the *imago De*i (the image of God):

> "When we reflect on the fact that Christ is the perfect image of God, we see an important relationship between the image of God and the Incarnation. Would it have been possible for the Second Person of the Trinity to assume the nature of an animal? This does not seem likely. The Incarnation means that the Word who was God became flesh—that is, assumed the nature of man (Jn. 1:14). That God could become flesh is the greatest of all mysteries, which will always transcend our finite human understanding. But, presumably, it was only because man had been created in the image of God that the Second Person of the Trinity could assume human nature. That Second Person, it would seem, could not have assumed a nature that had no resemblance whatever to God. In other words, the Incarnation confirms the doctrine of the image of God."[134]

Hoekema's point is powerful because it means Adam and Eve were created in the image of God *because* of Jesus Christ! Christ coming, in the likeness of man and taking on human nature, was always part of God's eternal will (cf. Jn. 17.4-5). We should point to a few more examples of Christ in the Old Testament to show how Scripture has always anticipated its Christocentric revelatory apex and its highest redemptive point in Christ and His cross-work.

Jesus is also found in God's promise to Adam and Eve in His post-lapsarian pronouncement of blessing and curse:

Genesis 3:14–15 [14] "The Lord God said to the serpent, "Because you have done this, Cursed are you more than all cattle, And more than every beast of the field; On your belly you will go, And dust you will eat All the days of your life; [15] And I will put enmity Between you and the woman, And between your seed

---

[134]Anthony A. Hoekema, *Created in God's Image* (Grand Rapids: Eerdmans, 1994), p.22.

and her seed; He shall bruise you on the head, And you shall bruise him on the heel."

This was the first time God gave a promise of cosmic victory over all sin and satanic influence. This victory would move a new humanity beyond the probation of innocence, beyond conflict with the serpent, and beyond the original (fallen) created order to the new creation where they would have access to the sacramental tree of life (Rev. 22.2). Consequently, it was in the coming of the *seed* that Adam and Eve would place their hope (e.g. Gen. 4.1).[135] The reference to this *seed*, and the redemptive promise contained in it, was reiterated throughout Genesis and finally spoken to Abraham in the context of a covenant which God ratified through a sovereign unconditional ritual that assured the certainty of God's promises to Abraham, that all nations would be blessed in connection to him (Gen. 15). The fact that *all* nations would be blessed by virtue of their connection to Abraham and his *seed* is explained in Galatians 3 where Paul clearly identifies the *seed* as Abraham's ultimate singular messianic *Seed*, that is Jesus Christ; *He* would bring all of God's redemptive promises to pass (cf. 2 Cor. 1.20):

> **Galatians 3:15–18** [15] "Brethren, I speak in terms of human relations: even though it is only a man's covenant, yet when it has been ratified, no one sets it aside or adds conditions to it. [16] Now the promises were spoken to Abraham and to his seed. He does not say, "And to seeds," as referring to many, but rather to one, "And to your seed," that is, Christ. [17] What I am saying is this: the Law, which came four hundred and thirty years later, does not invalidate a covenant previously ratified by God, so as to nullify the promise. [18] For if the inheritance is based on law, it is no longer based on a promise; but God has granted it to Abraham by means of a promise."

---

[135]In Gen. 4.1 commentators have detected hope in Eve's much debated proclamation, "I have gotten a manchild with the help of the Lord." The phrase seems to suggest that Eve may have thought the promise of (3.15) was to be fulfilled with the arrival of Cain. For more on this point see, Victor P. Hamilton, *The New International Commentary on the Old Testament, The Book of Genesis Chapters 1-17* (Grand Rapids/Cambridge: Eerdmans, 1990) p.221. Clowney also draws out many of the implications, fulfillments and theological points of agreement between the Garden event and the theology it ushers in within the New Testament; see, Edmund P. Clowney, *The Unfolding Mystery, Discovering Christ in the Old Testament* (Phillipsburg: P&R, 1988) pp. 35-42

From the primeval history of God's people, to the formation of God's *chosen* people in the wilderness, God had given His people true hope of final redemption through His Seed, His Deliverer, His Prophet, His Lamb, and His Anointed One. Throughout Israel's long history of travail and tribulation, God was surrounding His people with one reminder or symbol of future redemption after another. From the propitiation symbolized in the Passover, to the holiness demanded in the sacrificial system, the possessing and seeing the glory of God in the tabernacle and temple, to the deliverance and re-gathering of God's exiles in Assyria and Babylon—all things were pointing God's people towards the consummation of all these shadows and types. This is why the author of Hebrews saw such eschatological consummation in the cross, "now once at the consummation of the ages He has been manifested to put away sin by the sacrifice of Himself" (Heb. 9.26). The cross of Christ is a *consummate* cross. As Ross notes, this was all part of God's eternal "plan of redemption":

> "...for centuries God was teaching people important theological aspects about his eternal plan. When the Son of God came into the world to fulfill this plan, a treasure of theological images and ideas was ready at hand. People knew exactly what God meant by sacrifice, because the Spirit of God had taught it to and through Israel in the revelation of the sacrifices and offerings. People understood what was meant by atonement, purification, or consecration because the people of God had been living out these rituals for centuries. People were fully aware of the differences between clean and unclean or between holy and unholy because those categories had been applied to every detail of life for as long as folks could remember. By the time of Jesus, sacrifices, rituals, festivals, and all of the Levitical procedures were at the center of Israel's way of life."[136]

To borrow the language of Hebrews, "time would fail me" to point out every instance in which Christological anticipation is foreshadowed in the OT. The Passover was to be kept in remembrance of God's deliverance from Egypt, but also in anticipation of God's future propitious sacrifice in Christ—the ultimate Passover Lamb (1 Cor. 5.7). This ancient commemoration symbolized, not only, escaping the wrath of Egypt, but

---

[136]Allen P. Ross, *Holiness to the Lord, A Guide to the Exposition of the Book of Leviticus* (Grand Rapids: Baker Academic, 2002) p.17.

God's wrath through the cross where the ultimate blood would be applied to God's people making it possible for *eternal* death to pass by (cf. Jn. 3.14-15). The Passover did not merely remove the terror of God's wrath negatively, it also was efficacious in that it represented the positive righteousness of Christ who, not only, atones for us, and in that sense passes over us, but He also qualifies us as the people of God through His own righteousness.

The Sacrificial System also pointed to the cross. God literally surrounded the Jewish Nation with the cross-work of Christ by inundating them with symbolic practices that longed for their corresponding realities—a reality only that Christ Himself could provide (cf. Col. 2.16-17). As Ross points out, all sacrifices were pregnant with Christology for they prefigured and revealed the way God would make man acceptable to Him by faith alone, in Christ alone:

> "In ancient Israel, faith was demonstrated by bringing the sacrifice and placing a hand on it. In the church today a Christian is someone who has appropriated the sacrifice of Christ by faith and is therefore said to be "in Christ." Consequently, Christians have favor with God because of the merits of the shed blood of the Lamb of God. This is the eternal plan of God, revealed first in the law of the burnt offering and fulfilled in the sacrificial death of the Messiah, namely, that all who draw near to God on the basis of this atoning sacrifice made once and for all have been accepted by God, forever."[137]

Every drop of blood and every offering at the altar was intended to stir within God's people a need for one ultimate sacrifice that would put an end to all other sacrifices and do away with the blood of bulls and goats once and for all (Heb. 9.13-14; 10.1-4). As a token to the fact that Christ did in fact fulfill all that the sacrificial institutions called for, the author of Hebrews says, "but He, having offered one sacrifice for sins for all time, *sat down* at the right hand of God" (Heb. 10.12). Where as in all other temple or tabernacle situations, the Levitical priests never were to sit down since sacrifices in the OT never ended, Jesus *sat down*. In contrast to all priests who came before Him, Jesus' priestly role is also *regal* in nature. He is the Messiah and Priest, but also *King*. Indeed He

---

[137]Ibid. pp.96-97.

is *the enthroned priest*[138] of God's people. Thus, it was precisely through His priestly work of offering Himself as the ultimate sacrifice of sin that Christ would assume His exalted station at the right hand of God following His resurrection (cf. Acts 2.29-31).

Likewise, God's covenants also powerfully spoke of Christ. Every bond God made with His people had a Christological emphasis. Like His Laws and institutions, God's covenants produced great Messianic anticipation. The blessing of the nations promised and sealed in sacred bond with Abraham, the giving of the Law through Moses at Sinai (where the need for perfect righteousness on the part of God's covenant people was revealed), and the Davidic promise of an everlasting throne which would never fail to be filled, all prefigured the only One which could bring about the *substance* of the *shadows*, the delivery and affirmation of the promises (2 Cor. 1.20), and the consummation of all things (Eph. 1.11; Heb. 9.26).

As we reflect on all of the precious shadows God gave His people in order to anticipate Christ; such shadows must never outshine the substance. As one author pointed out, "The 'husk' of externalities had a useful purpose. But now that the reality has appeared in history, insistence on continuation of the husk-forms insults and nullifies the reality."[139] After all, it is the cross that must take *center stage* in God's redemptive drama. Dennis Johnson points this out as he reminds us that Jesus is in fact the center of God's redemptive saga. This leads us to interpret Scripture in a Christocentric fashion which binds the book of God together. Far from being a "one-stringed guitar", Christ-centered hermeneutics only serves to show us the vast and radical Christ-centeredness of God himself and the Christ-centered nature of Biblical revelation and therefore the centrality of the *cross*:

> "This shows us that to walk with Jesus through the varied terrain of his Word and the diverse eras of God's redemptive history is not to strum a one-stringed guitar! To be sure, Jesus' cross and resurrection take center stage in the true, historical drama of God's great and costly rescue adventure. But just as

---

[138]Peter T. O'Brien, *The Letter to the Hebrews, The Pillar New Testament Commentary* (Grand Rapids, MI; Nottingham, England: Eerdmans, 2010) p.355.

[139]O Palmer Robertson, *The Christ of the Covenants* (Philipsburg: P&R, 1980) p.60.

Jesus traveled the breadth of the Bible—Law, Prophets, Writings—to show his friends its disclosure of his person and saving mission, he showed them the fullness of blessing that would flow from his sacrificial death and resurrection triumph. The multidimensional effects of his accomplishment of redemption are reflected throughout Israel's Scriptures. We are rebellious and guilty, needing repentance and forgiveness. Both are found in Jesus' name, through faith in him. The human race is a beautiful rainbow of many nationalities and ethnic groups, yet our sinful pride and suspicion turn our diversity into a breeding ground for division and conflict. Israel's Scriptures forecast the fulfillment of God's ancient promise to Abraham, to bring blessing and unity to "all the families of the earth" (Gen. 12:3), in a glorious reconciliation effected by Christ… When we read the Bible through the lens of Jesus Christ, we begin to glimpse an astonishing display an array of wisdom, mercy, and power. We see how "the manifold grace of God" (1 Pet. 4:10 NASB; see Eph. 3:10) radiates in all directions from the beloved eternal Son who became the well-pleasing incarnate Son, who was rejected as the curse-bearing Son for others, and who now lives and rules in glory as the exalted Son and who dwells with his people by his Spirit."[140]

Therefore, when we come to the New Testament, what we find is that all of these prefigures, shadows and forecasts of Jesus were not simply interpreted messianically, but progressively and redemptively, i.e. involving Christ's sufferings, sacrifice and salvation as the redemptive climax of God's eternal plan (Eph. 3.9-11). As Peter reflects on the promises contained and communicated through the prophets, he does not hesitate to identify their *prophecies* as redemptive in nature—focusing on Christ and His cross:

1 Peter 1:10–12 [10] "As to this salvation, the prophets who prophesied of the grace that would come to you made careful searches and inquiries, [11] seeking to know what person or time the Spirit of Christ within them was indicating as He predicted the sufferings of Christ and the glories to follow. [12] It was revealed to them that they were not serving themselves, but you,

---

[140]Dennis E. Johnson, *Walking with Jesus Through His Word: Discovering Christ In All The Scriptures* (Philipsburg, NJ: P&R Publishing, 2015) pp. 14-15.

in these things which now have been announced to you through those who preached the gospel to you by the Holy Spirit sent from heaven—things into which angels long to look."

As old rituals are fulfilled and set aside (cf. Heb. 8.13), new ones are graciously given. What they have in common is that neither can be understood apart from the cross. The structure of Scripture not only reveals anticipation of Christ and the cross on the prophetic horizon, it also results in reflection and remembrance of that greatest of all redemptive events. God's people are to forever look back to the cross and in doing so they are to savor the person and work of Christ.

Ordinances

We move from the fact that God is indeed gathering to Himself a new humanity in and through the cross—that which God's OT people had been eagerly awaiting; to the fact that God sets within the church various markers to remind us of the cross itself. Now that the OT shadows and types have been fulfilled in Christ, the New Covenant believer stands in a better place in redemptive history. We have a great advantage in the New Covenant in that we have a closed canon, newly constituted people/church, spiritual boldness, and a redemptive vantage point that helps to cement the centrality of the cross in the panoply of the meta-narrative of Scripture.[141] Just as the Old Covenant people of God were given various signs which pointed them to the cross, the New Covenant also gives us ordinances which remind us of the cross-centered nature of our Christian lives. We will consider Baptism, the Lord's Supper and Christian Leadership in order to see this cross-centered emphasis in the NT.

Immersed In The Cross

Baptism is such a glorious and sweet reminder of the work of the cross that we must stop and marvel at its meaning. As a pastor I have had the immense privilege of performing many baptisms. I have always accompa-

---

[141] By "meta-narrative" I simply refer to the story line or story-structure of Scripture. "Story" or "narrative" are useful terms not only for studying Biblical Theology but also for seeing the organic nature of all of the various parts of Scripture. Unlike the word, "history" a metanarrative helps us to see the interrelated nature of the whole Bible since often historical events in world history may or may not have anything to do with each other but in Scripture, every event is somehow organically connected and ultimately Christologically designed.

nied the preaching of the cross with baptism in order to show that the cross gives meaning to the ordinance itself. The principle passage that brings the cross and the ordinance of baptism together is Romans 6. Here we are told that our lives should be found worthy of the reality represented in baptism, namely that, "our old self was crucified with Him" (Rom. 6.6). Baptism is an exposition of the gospel without words. That is what ordinances/ sacraments are; they are voiceless sermons preached through acting out of a holy institution. Both baptism and the Lord's Supper are a matter of life and death:

> **Romans 6:1–7** [1] "What shall we say then? Are we to continue in sin so that grace may increase? [2] May it never be! How shall we who died to sin still live in it? [3] Or do you not know that all of us who have been baptized into Christ Jesus have been baptized into His death? [4] Therefore we have been buried with Him through baptism into death, so that as Christ was raised from the dead through the glory of the Father, so we too might walk in newness of life. [5] For if we have become united with Him in the likeness of His death, certainly we shall also be in the likeness of His resurrection, [6] knowing this, that our old self was crucified with Him, in order that our body of sin might be done away with, so that we would no longer be slaves to sin; [7] for he who has died is freed from sin."

Baptism is a symbol of the cross's power to kill what is *earthly* in us (cf. Col. 3.5). This is why walking in sin after baptism (primarily spiritual baptism) is a complete contradiction to the gospel. If we live in a state of impenitent disobedience, after receiving the knowledge of the truth in conversion, we lie about what the gospel has done for us. Death to sin is Paul's assumption since a baptism into *death* has taken place. This death-baptism is the ramification of our Christ-baptism, "all of us who have been baptized into Christ Jesus have been baptized into His death" (Rom. 6.3). In a sense, these are appositional statements meaning that they refer to the same phenomenon although they emphasize different angles of our union with Christ. Being "baptized into Christ Jesus",[142] means that we have been identified with the death of Christ because it

---

[142]Gk: ἐβαπτίσθημεν εἰς Χριστὸν Ἰησοῦν. The use of the Passive voice for "baptized" (ἐβαπτίσθημεν) is probably to be taken generally as a Divine Passive with the theological implications of the Spirit's role as the Divine agent who puts us into Christ's body (cf. 1 Cor. 12.13). The Spirit baptizes us into Christ!

is through His death, through the cross, that our union with Christ is made possible. But the cross does not only lead to death and burial, but also to life and peace, "Therefore we have been buried with Him through baptism into death, so that as Christ was raised from the dead through the glory of the Father, so we too might walk in newness of life" (Rom. 6.4). This new life is gloriously depicted when we emerge from the waters of baptism. It is a corporate reminder to the church of what took place in their own life and constitutes a truly wonderful opportunity to reflect on what our present spiritual condition is as we witness others being baptized. It also symbolizes our victory in Christ. Thus, the cross is not only the emblem of death, but also of life and victory over sin and death. The cross is a *sanctifying* cross. It causes us to live a divine analogy where we parallel Jesus' death and life as we come into spiritual union with Him. That is what is symbolically depicted in the ordinance of baptism.

Baptism should be an emotional time. After all, we are celebrating a person's death and resurrection, that is, we are acknowledging the horrible things we have done; the sin, the pride, the ungodliness and unrighteousness that once threatened to undo us (cf. Eph. 2.1-3). Furthermore, we also celebrate resurrection life, newness of life, and a new creation (cf. 2 Cor. 5.17). The cross is a *new-creational cross.*[143] Through baptism we are saying that the cross has the power to take us out of the chaos and disorder of our sinful misery and bring us into the beauty of a new life and new creation where we are being restored back into the image of our Creator one degree of glory at a time (2 Cor. 3.18; Col. 3.10[144]). Baptism sets before us the sin-shattering power of the cross that kills us before it makes us alive again—setting us free from the dominion of sin (Rom. 6.1-7). Seeing a sinner, once hell-bound, hell-bent enter the waters of baptism in order to proclaim the life-imparting power of the cross is a genuine means of grace for the soul of the whole church. Through baptism[145] we are immersed in the power of the cross to deliver us from the mastery of sin. In fact, baptism should remind us

---

[143]The phrase, "new-creational" is found in G.K. Beale's, *A New Testament Biblical Theology* (Grand Rapids: Baker, 2011).

[144]Notice also the "new-creational" language in Col. 3.9-10 with the "old" and "new self" and its cross-centered parallel in Rom. 6.6, "our old self was *crucified* with Him."

[145]In speaking of what takes place "through baptism" or "in baptism" I am not so much referring to a strict causal aspect, I am assuming the precedence of conversion and thus, spiritual baptism depicted by the water.

of the totality of death that the cross entails until we arrive at the extent of its new-creational power:

> **Galatians 6:14–15** [14] "But may it never be that I would boast, except in the cross of our Lord Jesus Christ, through which the world has been crucified to me, and I to the world. [15] For neither is circumcision anything, nor uncircumcision, but a new creation."

Negatively, the cross also crucifies the *world* to us and us *to the world* so that several *deaths* can be said to transpire here: the death of Jesus, "the cross of our Lord Jesus Christ", the death of believers with Jesus, "through which",[146] the death of the world[147] to believers, "the world has been crucified to me", and the death of believers to the world, "and I to the world." It is the total breaking away with the world and with sin and the total reorientation of life in a "new creation." As a person goes down into the waters of baptism, what is symbolized in the ordinance is the old order of things i.e. the old man, the old life, the old creation etc. As we emerge from the water the symbolism of baptism speaks to the "newness of life" in a virtual foretaste of life in the new creation where God's people will walk according to a new rule a new life principle of our union with Christ and our conformity to the kingdom of God. This rule allows us to live radically different lives in the present evil age through a habitual contemplation of our crucified status where we say with Paul, "I have been crucified with Christ" (Gal. 2.20 cf. Phil. 3.10). Baptism reflects our entrance into that status, but it also symbolizes the commitment we make to live a life of repentant obedience (cf. Rom. 6.17). For many people today, getting baptized is a mere formality, a point of peer pressure during youth camp, or an emotional response to a pastor's plea during an evangelistic rally. When we are immersed in the waters of baptism, we are immersing ourselves into the total Christian experience; a whole new identity. But baptism is serious business. We are committing to take up an arduous cross that calls us to daily death. During baptism we should be ready to embrace the cross-centered command that Jesus often gave to His disciples:

---

[146]This prepositional phrase, δι' οὗ, is conveying the reality of our Union with Christ. Because we are united to Christ in His crosswork, the world is now dead or *crucified* to us.

[147]Of course here, the "world" is referring to the evil system of anti-Christ standards, ethics, morals, reason, and spirituality.

Luke 9:23–26 [23] "And He was saying to them all, "If anyone wishes to come after Me, he must deny himself, and take up his cross daily and follow Me. [24] For whoever wishes to save his life will lose it, but whoever loses his life for My sake, he is the one who will save it. [25] For what is a man profited if he gains the whole world, and loses or forfeits himself? [26] For whoever is ashamed of Me and My words, the Son of Man will be ashamed of him when He comes in His glory, and the glory of the Father and of the holy angels."

Matthew 10:37–39 [37] "He who loves father or mother more than Me is not worthy of Me; and he who loves son or daughter more than Me is not worthy of Me. [38] And he who does not take his cross and follow after Me is not worthy of Me. [39] He who has found his life will lose it, and he who has lost his life for My sake will find it."

Baptism does not simply speak about our decisive break with sin, it also represents the cost of discipleship. For many of us today following Jesus does not cost us much. We come and go as we please, we join churches and leave churches at a whim, we know very little of commitment to the community of believers at the local church, and we get easily bored, bothered, and bitter. Baptism calls us to die to self! The truth is that often the profundity of the cross is found in the most practical ways. The cross calls us to deny self and remain faithful in a fickle and faithless world. No one understood that better than our selfless Redeemer who was committed to be crucified for us (cf. Phil. 2.1-11).

Feasting On The Cross

It has always amazed me that God in His sovereign wisdom only gave the church two ordinances—*Baptism* and the *Lord's Supper*. But as we pause to think of the symbolic meaning of each ordinance, we quickly see that God gave us a sacramental abundance of cross-centered vestiges to inform and enlarge our hearts in worship. Such is the case with the Lord's Supper. If the ordinance of baptism immerses us in the cross, the Lord's Supper is our time to internalize the cross by feasting on the cross-work of Jesus by faith. Jesus often perplexed the people by speaking of "eating His flesh" and "drinking His blood" (Jn. 6.53). In the context of John 6, Jesus has given the disciples several metaphors relating to *faith*. He is the bread that has come out of heaven to give us life (Jn. 6.32-33, 48). The metaphor of *coming* to Jesus also serves to illustrate the need to place personal trust in Jesus for redemption (Jn. 6.36). The same is true for seeing or *beholding* the Son of God. *Seeing* Jesus with the eye of faith results in "eternal life" (Jn. 6.40). John 6 is a metaphor-rich chapter that calls us to fix and anchor our trust and hope in Jesus who was sent to us from Heaven:

> **John 6:52–58** [52] "Then the Jews began to argue with one another, saying, "How can this man give us His flesh to eat?" [53] So Jesus said to them, "Truly, truly, I say to you, unless you eat the flesh of the Son of Man and drink His blood, you have no life in yourselves. [54] He who eats My flesh and drinks My blood has eternal life, and I will raise him up on the last day. [55] For My flesh is true food, and My blood is true drink. [56] He who eats My flesh and drinks My blood abides in Me, and I in him. [57] As the living Father sent Me, and I live because of the Father, so he who eats Me, he also will live because of Me. [58] This is the bread which came down out of heaven; not as the fathers ate and died; he who eats this bread will live forever."

Although this passage comes earlier than the institution of the Lord's Supper, and therefore is not referring to communion directly, it certainly captures the essence of putting our personal trust in Christ's work on the cross. The Lord's Supper reminds us of the importance of what we are trusting in, the flesh (broken) and blood (shed) for us on the cross. The Lord's Supper goes further than merely internalizing the body and blood of Jesus by faith. In the Supper, that body is *broken*, and that blood is *poured* out for us sacrificially, vicariously, and covenantally:

> **Luke 22:19–20** [19] "And when He had taken some bread and given thanks, He broke it and gave it to them, saying, "This is My body which is given for you; do this in remembrance of Me." [20] And in the same way He took the cup after they had eaten, saying, "This cup which is poured out for you is the new covenant in My blood."

This is yet another way that God has built a cross-centered vision into the very *molecular* structure of the Church. We cannot forget the cross in the Church because the bread and the cup were broken and poured out on the cross. Taking the bread into our hands and putting the cup to our lips is an intimate reminder that the Savior who has died for us is also ever with us.

Remembering the cross through the Lord's Supper is also something we do *corporately*. Churches that encourage their people to initiate the rite in their private home lives, or even worse, in total individual isolation completely miss the purpose of the Supper. The Supper is done when the saints gather in the context of the church so that they are reminded why they have gathered together as a church in the first place (cf. 1 Cor. 11.18, 17-22). Partaking of this sacred ordinance in isolation from the body of Christ is, in fact, a complete contradiction to the Supper itself; after all, eating supper alone is unnatural. We are meant to feast as the family of God.

In our Church, we regularly partake of the Supper and when we do so, we usually read from the central New Testament passage that gives the most detailed instructions for how the Supper is to be taken:

> **1 Corinthians 11:23–26** [23] "For I received from the Lord that which I also delivered to you, that the Lord Jesus in the night in which He was betrayed took bread; [24] and when He had given thanks, He broke it and said, "This is My body, which is for you; do this in remembrance of Me." [25] In the same way He took the cup also after supper, saying, "This cup is the new covenant in My blood; do this, as often as you drink it, in remembrance of Me." [26] For as often as you eat this bread and drink the cup, you proclaim the Lord's death until He comes."

The ordinance is meant to bring back the drama of Jesus' crucifixion. Notice that Paul adds a very specific detail in his communion instructions, "in the night in which He was betrayed" (1 Cor. 11.23). This draws us back into the drama of the events leading up to the cross. He is in effect tracing back the steps that lead to the cross. The Lord's Supper draws us into the narrative of the cross to remind us of the active obedience of a perfect Savior and the passive obedience of a perfect sacrifice. That should be what flashes before our minds: the betrayal, the Sanhedrin, Gethsemane, the arrest and trial, beatings, and crucifixion. Like baptism, the Lord's Supper should be an emotional time for those who genuinely treasure the gospel. Sadly, the context of the Corinthian passage reveals a lack of reverence on behalf of the church's members.

They had turned the Supper into a mockery by engaging in selfish greed and even drunkenness (1 Cor. 11.21-22). The supper was also neglected to the point that Paul made the shocking claim that some were so severely disciplined that they died as a result! Because of neglect, Paul says, "many among you are weak and sick, and a number sleep" (1 Cor. 11.30). The Church, by its sin, unworthy conduct and attitudes, and neglect were sending the wrong message about the importance of the Supper. Like baptism, the Lord's Supper conveys many messages and central among those messages is "the Lord's death", "For as often as you eat this bread and drink the cup, you proclaim the Lord's death until He comes" (1 Cor. 11.26).

Getting the church together for one unified purpose can often be challenging for leaders; but in the Lord's Supper, God masterfully, and in His sovereign wisdom, unites the church's evangelistic voice to "proclaim the Lord's death until He comes." As Charles Hodge points out, this proclamation should be our "definite purpose" in the Supper:

> "Those who come to it, therefore should come not to satisfy hunger, nor for the gratification of social feelings, but for the definite purpose of bearing their testimony to the great fact of redemption, and to contribute their portion of influence to the preservation and propagation of the knowledge of that fact."[148]

Servants of the Cross

Among other things, the ordinances of the church serve to remind us of the importance of the local church and of having our Christian life lived out in ecclesiastical community with other spirit-filled believers. We live in such an anti-church culture in post-modern, post-Christian America today that we need to remind ourselves of the centrality of the church. The church must be woven into the very fabric of all Christian life. There is a desperate need for the church to reclaim institutional authority, as that edifice of ecclesiastical rule, which Christ Himself instituted on planet Earth (Mt. 16.18-19). People think church is man's idea not God's, but the church is God's idea from the very beginning, indeed from eternity (cf. Eph. 3.9-11). Largely, in part to the anti-doctrinal sentiments of the Jesus Movement in the sixties, the church has had

---

[148]Charles Hodge, *1 & 2 Corinthians, Geneva Series of Commentaries* (Edinburgh/Carlisle: Banner of Truth Trust, 2000) 229.

to gnaw and claw its way back to a high view of the local church as more than simply the building next to the boys and girls club down the street, which basically engages in the same sorts of activities anyways. Carl Henry pointed out this precise anti-intellectual shift in the Evangelical church many years ago:

> "For all its thrust beyond the evangelical establishment churches, the Jesus movement tends to be intellectually shallow and doctrinally tolerant, accommodating subbiblical and even heretical concepts for the sake of "Christian love." In different places the Christ of the Jesus movement was the Dropout Carpenter interested in the invisible world, the Leader of a Commune on a nomadic pilgrimage, the Critic of the Establishment, and undoubtedly for a goodly number the Strong Son of God who proffers divine salvation to repentant sinners."[149]

Affecting, not only, the doctrine of salvation and Christology, the anti-intellectualism from which much of the modern contemporary church sprung (conscientiously or not) affects both soteriology and *ecclesiology*. As *fragmented* as the church may be as a result of its historical upheavals and trends, Henry gives us sound sagacity when he counsels the way forward from what he called, "the highly individualistic mood of American evangelicalism":

> "Evangelical Christians in their fragmented condition no less than ecumenical Christians in their structural affiliation seem to lack the realization that Christ's church is to be a "new community" united in love for God and neighbor and identifiably functioning in the world as light and salt. Such a corporate fellowship of believers will have a vanguard of scholars to exhibit the truth of revelation with an intellectual power that confronts non-Christian ideologies; it will have a biblically rooted laity that withstands the heresies of the age; a mature lay leadership that takes Christian initiatives, counsels the burdened, and ministers to the needy. It will bring both male and female and the Christian home fully into the experience of Chris-

---

[149]Carl Ferdinand Howard Henry, *God, Revelation, and Authority; vol.1*, (Wheaton, IL: Crossway Books, 1999) p.132

[150]Ibid. Vol. 1, p.133.

tian fulfillment. And above all it will as a community be committed to Christ in radical discipleship, exhibiting God's truth, love and righteousness in personal and public dimensions."[150]

It is precisely this type of leadership that will be required to bring the church back to its cross-centered roots. The church has a duty to explain the sacramental importance of its practices and how they relate to the soul of the gospel—*the cross*. When this is done, as Henry noted, then we will have "a biblically rooted laity that withstands the heresies of the age", for those heresies are many and metastasizing as we speak! For the church that does not have an aversion to doctrinal specificity, institutionalism, formalism, and structure, God has graciously given us yet another tremendous means of cross-centeredness—the servant-leaders of the cross.

The leaders of the Church are to be servants of the cross, who lift up the cross in their respective ministries, irrespective of popular opinion and even pragmatic pressure from within the church, who center their ministries on something other than the gospel and the curse-bearing cross of Jesus. Pastors bear such an enormous responsibility to proclaim Christ as they officiate, like temple priests, at His altar before His people (cf. Rom. 15.16). Today the pressures placed on the pastors are extensive, complex and compromised. It is a call to infuse more media into the sermons, more technology into the service, more personality into the delivery, more fashion onto the stage, more causes into the agenda, more youthfulness into the atmosphere, more juvenile humor, more therapy into the worship, and more psychology into the counseling. But, as God's revelation stands, the emphasis is unapologetically on the *cross*. "I determined to knowing among you except Jesus Christ, and Him crucified" (1 Cor. 2.2). Thus, our sermons should be dripping with the blood of the cross, stressing the power of the cross to destroy sin and the wonder of the cross to transform us into cruciform Christians, who bear an indelible mark of crucified lives (Gal. 2.20; 6.14). The cross is the foundation of a biblically informed leadership, whose sole aim is to please the one who enlisted it for ministry in the first place (cf. 2 Tim. 2.4).

The shepherds of the church must strive to make their churches a fellowship that magnifies the corporate dimensions of the cross in the face of the culture's individualistic, anti-institutional idolatry. It is a *deep narcissism* that we are fighting in today's spiritual climate—a narcissism that can only be rooted out by the nails of a soul-altering cross (Lk. 23.43).

When the paradisiacal power of the cross comes into view, then the mirage of our narcissistic ways become clear. Only the riches of the cross possess the power to render our covetous and kleptomaniacal hearts changed enough to leave behind the fleeting pleasure of *Egyptian* sin, with its temporal rewards for the eternal riches of Christ (Heb. 11.26). Thieves and whores will declare Jesus as their sole Savior and Lord only as the cleansing power of the cross frees them from their bondage and sprinkles their conscience clean to steal and seduce no more (Jn. 4.16-17).

From another angle, it is also the power of the cross that gathers sinners from all walks and sits them around the table of a new household (cf. 1 Cor. 1.26f.). Our whole purpose for gathering together is owing to the cross. Our mission towards each other is fueled by the realities of the cross that have rendered us selfless servants of Jesus, who condescend to meet the needs of others even before ourselves (cf. Phil. 2.1-5). Just as Christ became as nothing for us through His condescension, Christian ministry is all about emptying us of self. The consciousness of the cross is selflessness. Such a cross-centered, self-denying, others-focused ministry will be a formidable challenge in our self-centered age. D. A. Carson points out the narcissistic challenges we face in Christian ministry:

> "The heart of our wretched rebellion is that each of us wants to be number one. We make ourselves the center of all our thoughts and hopes and imaginations. This vicious lust to be first works its way outward not only in hatred, war, rape, greed, covetousness, malice, bitterness, and much more, but also in self-righteousness, self-promotion, manufactured religions, and domesticated gods… Our self-centeredness is deep. It is so brutally idolatrous that it tries to domesticate God himself. In our desperate folly we act as if we can outsmart God, as if he owes us explanations, as if we are wise and self-determining while he exists only to meet our needs."[151]

Every ministry of the church should be designed in a selfless, cruciform shape. In other words, the implications of the cross define everything we do in the church; *how we pray*, broken, humble, and contrite in recognition of the grace shown to us at the cross; *how we sing*, with hearts

---

[151]D.A. Carson, *The Cross and Christian Ministry, Leadership Lessons from 1 Corinthians* (Grand Rapids: Baker, 2004) pp.14-15.

made glad by the sheer power of the cross to bear the curse for us, remove God's wrath from us, and impart forgiveness and life to us for the glory of the triune God; *how we give*, knowing that God gave us His indescribable gift to teach us to be generous beyond our means so that in fact we become greedy for generosity (2 Cor. 8.3; 9.15); *how we teach*, knowing that the cross is the wisdom of God, apart from which our wisdom is rendered as nothing more than dark futile folly (1 Cor. 1.18-21); *how we evangelize*, seeing that we have no greater message than Christ crucified (1 Cor. 2.2: see Ch. 7 below); *how we participate*, faithfully recognizing that Jesus died for the church and purchased the church with His own blood (Acts 20.28) so that we would value the church even as God does and dare not neglect it (Heb. 10.25). These are merely some of the corporate dimensions of the cross; dimensions that the Church's leaders are duty-bound to proclaim and prescribe (cf. Tit. 2.15). It all begins with preaching the cross. It is the cross that can make the church a thriving church.

As servants of the cross, specifically those tasked with preaching and teaching, the essence of Christian proclamation reaches the soul of the gospel through its preaching and unfolding of the various dimensions of the cross-centered nature of Christian theology.[152] The apostles in their preaching and their writing were dominated by the theology of the cross. Leon Morris makes this point clear in his great work on *The Cross in the New Testament*:

"… The cross dominates the New Testament. Notice how naturally it is referred to as summing up the content of Christianity. 'We preach Christ crucified' (1 Cor. 1:23); 'I determined not to know anything among you, save Jesus Christ and him crucified' (1 Cor. 2:2); 'I delivered unto you first of all…how that Christ died for our sin' (1 Cor. 15:3); 'far be it from me to glory, save in the cross of our Lord Jesus Christ' (Gal. 6:14). The

---

[152]Scripture has many emphasis, however, there is no greater emphasis in Scripture than *Christ*. The cross is indissolubly connected to the Christocentric *loci* of Scripture. The motif of the cross is as central to Scripture as the motif of Christ (see, Lk. 24.27ff.). The emphasis in Luke, and other places (e.g. 1 Pet. 1.11) is not simply on Christ, but on Christ and His *sufferings* (Lk. 24.26). Of course, many of the NT texts are directly reflecting OT theology which only serves to illustrate further the Christocentric, and thus cross-centered, nature of Scripture from beginning to end. On this point see, Graeme Goldsworthy, *Christ-centered Biblical Theology: Hermeneutical Foundations and Principles* (Downers Grove: IVP. 2012).

Gospel is 'the word of the cross' (1 Cor. 1:18). The enemies of Christianity are 'the enemies of the cross of Christ (Phil. 3:18). Baptism is baptism into Christ's death (Rom. 6:3), and it is not without interest that, while Christ did not enjoin His followers to commemorate His birth, or any event in His life, He did call on them to remember His death. While it may not be expressly the theme in every place, yet it is because of the cross that every writer writes as he does."[153]

If the New Testament writers were dominated by the cross in what they wrote and did, so ought we. Finally, to see the utter cross-centeredness of New Testament ministry, we must look carefully and meaningfully at the central passage that gave birth to the present volume.

---

[153]Leon Morris, *The Cross in the New Testament* (Grand Rapids/Cambridge: Eerdmans, 1999) p.365.

7

CRUCIFIED FOR GOD'S GLORY, MAKING GOD THE CENTER THROUGH PREACHING THE CROSS

And when I came to you, brethren, I did not come with superiority of speech or of wisdom, proclaiming to you the testimony of God. 2 For I determined to know nothing among you except Jesus Christ, and Him crucified. 3 I was with you in weakness and in fear and in much trembling, 4 and my message and my preaching were not in persuasive words of wisdom, but in demonstration of the Spirit and of power, 5 so that your faith would not rest on the wisdom of men, but on the power of God.

1 Corinthians 2:1–5

In *Crucified: the Soul of the Gospel,* we have endeavored to show the cross-centered nature of the gospel, salvation and gospel ministry in the Church. We have looked at how preaching Christ means that we preach the implications of His cross-work without fear, not neglecting the precious truths of the sovereignty of God in election. We have also sought to make men sensible of their exceeding wickedness. The cross is central to this aspect of preaching the gospel. Too often the cross is thought to be auxiliary in making men sensible of their sinful misery. But we have seen how the cross shows man God's great displeasure for sin and the punishment that it incurred. The cross is also the instrument through which God reconciles hostile humanity to Himself, creating peace through the justifying power of the cross. Justification naturally bleeds into other aspects of the atonement, for example, substitution. The substitutionary aspect of the cross highlights the mercy of God in sending Christ to take our place, to die in our stead, and absorb the wrath of an infinitely holy God whom we have offended as sons and daughters of Adam. Without Christ placing Himself in harm's way for us, there is no propitiation and no way for sinners to be favored by God. Chapter five begins to show how Christ crucified is a message about *all* of life. The cross does not only represent initiation, but perpetual consecration, as Jesus sets us apart through our own cross-bearing life, for the glory of God in the context of sanctification. Chapter six serves to show how the cross and the Church go together. We cannot preach Christ without preaching the corporate dimensions of the cross. Finally, what remains is for a more focused exposition and exploration of the key text of this work, 1 Corinthians 2.2 where Paul says, "For I determined to know nothing among you except Jesus Christ, and Him crucified." The passage itself has a Theocentric, Christocentric and doxological thrust, that must be grasped if we are to understand Paul's relentless resolve to preach Christ's cross-work above all else. R.C. Sproul captures the inner thought of Paul's words here when he writes, "You might forget other things that I teach you, but don't ever forget the cross, because it was on the cross, through the cross and by the cross that our Savior performed His work of redemption and gathered His people for eternity."[154]

The Soul of the Gospel

The Corinthian letters are known for their controversial content especially as it relates to Paul's own relationship with the church and the church's slide into sin and theological compromise on various issues. Here (1 Cor. 2.1-5) Paul is reminding them of the all-important foundation which he laid down not only for the birthing of the church but for its future edification and upbuilding in grace and truth. So foundational, in fact, was Paul's preaching of the gospel or "Christ crucified", that Paul adds the emphatic resolve that he "determined to know nothing" among them "except Jesus Christ, and Him crucified." The terminus is on the word *crucified*, that is, the sacrifice that Jesus made on the cross on behalf of His people. Paul saw the resolve to preach Christ as foundational for the success and purity of the church itself:

> **1 Corinthians 3:10–15** [10] "According to the grace of God which was given to me, like a wise master builder I laid a foundation, and another is building on it. But each man must be careful how he builds on it. [11] For no man can lay a foundation other than the one which is laid, which is Jesus Christ. [12] Now if any

---

[154]R.C. Sproul, *The Truth of the Cross* (Orlando: Reformation Trust Publishing, 2007) p.5.

man builds on the foundation with gold, silver, precious stones, wood, hay, straw, [13] each man's work will become evident; for the day will show it because it is to be revealed with fire, and the fire itself will test the quality of each man's work. [14] If any man's work which he has built on it remains, he will receive a reward. [15] If any man's work is burned up, he will suffer loss; but he himself will be saved, yet so as through fire."

Too often the theological fidelity of the church is sidestepped by programs, music, or building projects, but for Paul this was not expendable. Sadly, many pastors are far more concerned with meeting people's felt needs, making sure they are likable, entertaining, humorous and culturally relevant rather than *biblical*. The result of getting away from preaching doctrine and carefully handling God's Word, by faithfully preaching the gospel is what Michael Horton called, "smooth talking and Christless Christianity."[155] It has resulted in a truly sad, narcissistic soulless and more important Christless, Christianity. Doctrine-lite churches feed into society's humanistic and autonomous idolatry. Horton wrote:

"We Americans are not well-known in the world as people who know how to blush. On the contrary, we are a very self-confident people. The last thing we want is to be told that we cannot do anything to save ourselves from the most serious problem that we have ever or will ever encounter—that we are entirely at God's mercy. Apart from a miracle, religious success in this atmosphere will always go to those who can effectively appeal to this can-do spirit and push as far to the background as possible anything that might throw our swaggering self off-balance. When looking for ultimate answers, we turn within ourselves, trusting our own experience rather than looking outside ourselves to God's external Word… Out of self-love, Paul warned Timothy, people will gather teachers who will tell them exactly what they want to hear (2 Tim. 3:2-4; 4:3-5). Much of what we call relevance Paul refers to in that passage as godlessness… "Smooth talk and flattery" is part of the staple diet of successful American religion today. And it is almost always advertised simply as more effective mission and relevance.[156]

---

[155]Michael Horton, *Christless Christianity*, p.66.

[156]Ibid, pp. 65-66.

Before moving on to what is said in 1 Corinthians 2 about the cross, we need to pause and consider *who* said it.[157] The apostle Paul was himself changed by the cross. The cross was an *experiential* cross for Paul (Gal. 6.17; Col. 1.24). He knew the power which he now proclaimed (cf. Phil. 3.10).[158] Paul was not only saved by the cross, he was shaped and sanctified by the cross.[159] For this reason, Paul can be called *the theologian of the cross.*[160] He wrote extensively on the cross; to the point that, as many have had to do, we can often only cite him in part.[161] Pauline theologians have often pointed out the centrality and magnitude of the cross in Paul's gospel. This led Leon Morris to confess, "The sheer bulk of Paul's teaching on the atonement makes it difficult to deal at all adequately with his thought."[162] Ridderbos says that "Jesus Christ and Him crucified" was in Paul the, "mystery of Christ", the "depths of God", that which God has purposed to Himself in Christ and has brought to revelation in the fullness of the time."[163] Having been so radically altered by the mystery of the cross, Paul saw himself as a steward of the mysteries of God (1 Cor. 4.1). More than a mystery, Paul saw that the revelation of God's mysteries in Christ redefined him; giving him a new *cruciform* identity:

> **Galatians 2:20** [20] "I have been crucified with Christ; and it is no longer I who live, but Christ lives in me; and the life which I now live in the flesh I live by faith in the Son of God, who loved me and gave Himself up for me."

---

[157] I have pointed out biographical details on Paul elsewhere, see, Emilio Ramos, *Convert from Adam to Christ*, (Alachua FL. Bridge-Logos . 2012).

[158] Acts 9.1-22; 1 Cor. 4.1; 2 Cor. 8.9; Col. 1.25; 1 Tim. 1.12-17.

[159] Rom. 6.4-6; 2 Cor. 1.5; 4.10-11; 12.9-10; Gal. 2.20; Phil. 3.10; 6.14; 2 Tim. 2.11-12.

[160] A phrase found in Luther's writings. See for example, Mr. Gerhard O. Forbe, *On Being a Theologian of the Cross: Reflections on Luther's Heidelberg Disputation*, 1518 (Grand Rapids: Eerdmans, 1997). Unlike Luther who had a more suffering-oriented use for the term, I use it to refer more broadly to the sheer exegetical theology found in the Pauline corpus dealing with the cross motif.

[161] See, Robert A. Peterson, *Salvation Accomplished by the Son: The Work of Christ* (Wheaton: Crossway, 2012) p.85. Peterson gives a sample of Paul's cross-saturated thought e.g. (Rom. 3.24-26; 4.25; 5.6-10; 6.3-10; 7.4; 8.2-4, 32, 34; 14.9, 15; 1 Cor. 1.17-18, 23; 2.2; 8.11; 10.16; 15.3, 14-15; 2 Cor. 4.10; 13.4; Gal. 2.20; 6.14; Eph. 1.7; 2.13-16; Phil. 2.8; 3.10; Col. 1.20, 22; 2.14, 20; 1 Thess. 4.14; 5.10; 2 Tim. 2.11, passim).

[162] Leon Morris, *The Cross in the New Testament*, 180.

[163] Herman Ridderbos, *Paul, An Outline of His Theology* (Grand Rapids: Eerdmans, 1992) p.244.

Galatians 6:14 [14] But may it never be that I would boast, except in the cross of our Lord Jesus Christ, through which the world has been crucified to me, and I to the world."

Philippians 3:7–11 [7] "But whatever things were gain to me, those things I have counted as loss for the sake of Christ. [8] More than that, I count all things to be loss in view of the surpassing value of knowing Christ Jesus my Lord, for whom I have suffered the loss of all things, and count them but rubbish so that I may gain Christ, [9] and may be found in Him, not having a righteousness of my own derived from the Law, but that which is through faith in Christ, the righteousness which comes from God on the basis of faith, [10] that I may know Him and the power of His resurrection and the fellowship of His sufferings, being conformed to His death; [11] in order that I may attain to the resurrection from the dead."

These texts tell us something of the changed consciousness of a man, recreated by the cross that killed him, in a spiritual sense (cf. Gal. 6.14). Paul's life having been reoriented by the cross, also demonstrates the all-encompassing implications it had for the apostle's total world and life view. Christ "crucified" represented, for Paul, the ultimate center of both Christian theology and preaching (cf. Acts 26.22-23; 28.23; Col. 1.28-29). This is why Paul, who himself had been shattered by the cross, was resolved to declare it unalloyed by human wisdom to a people who were inundated with philosophical sophistry of every kind. For Paul, the message of the cross brought unmatched clarity into a philosophically confused and chaotic world (Rom. 1.21; Eph. 4.17; Tit. 3.3).

As we approach the text itself, one must also see that this altruistic resolve was spoken in a context where the implications of the cross were, not only being challenged, but looked upon as utter folly (1 Cor. 1.18; 2.14; 4.10). Not only was Corinth (i.e. Corinthian) a byword for licentious living,[164] it was also the great hub of Greek philosophy. This is relevant because the cross is diametrically opposed to the philosophical musing of autonomous reason (Socratic or otherwise). In terms of Paul's interaction with the Corinthians, and the backdrop of 1 Corinthians, John MacArthur underscores the practical relevance of Paul's situation to our own today:

---

[164]Curtis Vaughan and Thomas D. Lea, *1 Corinthians* (Cape Coral: Founders Press, 2002) p.12.

"The general intent of what Paul is saying to the philosophically oriented Corinthians can be stated like this: "Since you have become Christians, have been filled by God's Spirit, and recognize the Scriptures as His Word, you have no more need for philosophy. It did not help you when you were unbelievers and it will certainly not help you now that you believe. Give it up. It has nothing to offer but confusion and division. You are now united around God's supreme revelation in Jesus Christ. Do not be misled and split by human speculations." Society in our own day still is enamored with various philosophies. These are not usually expressed in philosophical systems such as the Greeks had, but they are nevertheless human ways of understanding life's meaning and values and of understanding them. The world today, just as in Paul's day, is caught up in the admiration and worship of human opinion, human wisdom, and human desires and aspiration. Men are continually trying to figure out on their own what life is all about—where it came from, where it is going, what it signifies (if anything), and what can and should be done about it (if anything). Modern man has made gods of education and human opinion. Although human ideas are constantly changing, appearing and disappearing, being tried and found wanting, conflicting with and contradicting each other, men continue to put faith in them. As long as they reject divine authority, they have no other option…. Human wisdom, epitomized in philosophy, has always been a threat to revelation."[165]

This *threat* was current in Corinth, as it is in our own day. The Corinthians began taking heed to other foundational *principles* and *perspectives* on *knowledge*. The Corinthian culture was inundated with every kind of human rhetorical device, philosophy, and spirituality imaginable (cf. Acts 17.16). There were other maxims being presented to the church that threatened to replace Paul's all-important emphasis on the very heart and soul of the gospel contained in the message of the cross. As J.I. Packer has pointed out, without the cross there can be no Christianity:

"…where the Lord Jesus is not confessed as God incarnate, crucified, risen, reigning and returning, and where there is no focus

[165]John MacArthur Jr. (*1 Corinthians: The MacArthur New Testament Commentary*) pp. 36-37.

on the personal knowledge of Christ crucified, there is no Christianity."[166]

This means that no amount of philosophy, rhetoric or eloquence can replace the knowledge of the cross. Simply put, what Paul is arguing for here is the *preeminence* of the cross over all other forms of human wisdom as it relates to communicating the truth about who God is and what He has done for man in Christ. Paul's argument is that the message of the cross cannot be replaced or supplanted by human wisdom or, external signs, be they miracles or elsewise. And that the community of the cross (i.e. the Church) is not to be characterized by human wisdom over against the wisdom imparted to us by the Spirit of God since he who has the Spirit "appraises all things."[167] Thankfully in this text (i.e. 1 Cor. 2.2) Paul does not just assert the centrality of the cross, he argues for it with power and precision. We see several things in particular from the context of Paul's resolve and what Paul's cross-centered resolution was based on. To begin to see these exegetical points, we need to go back to chapter one and the broader context of the letter.

The Mission of God And The Centrality of The Cross

1 Corinthians 1:17 [17] "For Christ did not send me to baptize, but to preach the gospel, not in cleverness of speech, so that the cross of Christ would not be made void."

We should first begin by noticing the language of *mission* here, "For Christ did not *send me* to baptize."[168] Paul's opening statement is the occasion that leads to Paul's cross-centered resolve and the preaching of Christ crucified. For Paul, boasting in one's baptism (and in the person by whom you were baptized) was emptying the cross of its power and preeminence. The church began to become factious (1 Cor. 1.10-13). But Paul's mission was not focused on baptisms, but on making the cross of Jesus central, as the very wisdom and power of God (1 Cor. 1.24). Paul had a mandate not to count how many people he baptized personally, but how faithfully he preached the cross. It is on the basis of his *mandate*

---

[166]Stephen Charnock, *Christ Crucified: The Once for All Sacrifice* (Scotland UK: Christian Focus Publishing, 1996) p.10.

[167]1 Cor. 2.5a, ὁ δὲ πνευματικὸς ἀνακρίνει [τὰ] πάντα.

[168]οὐ γὰρ ἀπέστειλέν με Χριστὸς βαπτίζειν. It is also interesting to note that for Paul, Jesus was his direct Commissioner (cf. Acts 9.15).

that Paul was resolved to preach Christ crucified, "For Christ did not send me to baptize, but to preach the gospel" (1 Cor. 1.17). Whether pledging allegiance to a particular teacher or lauding an association with the minister who baptized them, the Corinthians were letting the vision and glory of the cross slip away.

This opening passage is a microcosm of the whole section, for in it Paul sets out the antithesis he is going to be developing. The reason why Paul wanted no other foundation for the church was because it was not compatible with God's cross-centered mission in the world. If Christ did not send Paul into the world to baptize, which is a good and necessary thing, there is nothing else which can take the place of preaching Christ.[169] This is the first reason Paul was resolved to preach Christ crucified; it was what God had commissioned him to do. Paul speaks of the same cross-centered emphasis for his ministry elsewhere:

> **Ephesians 3:8** [8] "To me, the very least of all saints, this grace was given, to preach to the Gentiles the unfathomable riches of Christ,"

> **1 Timothy 2:7** [7] "For this I was appointed a preacher and an apostle (I am telling the truth, I am not lying) as a teacher of the Gentiles in faith and truth."

> **2 Timothy 1:11** [11] "for which I was appointed a preacher and an apostle and a teacher."

> **1 Corinthians 15:10-11** [10] "But by the grace of God I am what I am, and His grace toward me did not prove vain; but I labored even more than all of them, yet not I, but the grace of God with me. [11] Whether then it was I or they, so we preach and so you believed."

Paul knew, and had come to understand, that it was through preaching that people would come to faith in Christ, "*we preach and so you be-*

---

[169]We should also notice Paul interchangeable use of the phrases "to preach the gospel" (εὐαγγελίζεσθαι) and "the word of the cross" ('Ο λόγος γὰρ ὁ τοῦ σταυροῦ) in 1.18, "we preach Christ" (κηρύσσομεν Χριστὸν) in 1.23, "proclaiming the testimony/ mystery of God" (καταγγέλλων ὑμῖν τὸ μυστήριον τοῦ θεοῦ) in 2.1, and "Jesus Christ, and Him crucified" (Ἰησοῦν Χριστὸν καὶ τοῦτον ἐσταυρωμένον) in 2.2. What this shows is that in all reality these phrases are virtually synonymous for Paul and refer to the gospel of Jesus Christ.

lieved." This also demonstrates the *sufficiency* of preaching the cross (cf. 2 Tim. 4.1-2). The sufficiency of preaching the gospel of the cross was now under attack at Corinth. The people were becoming distracted and even impressed with shiny rhetoric that did not possess the power of God unto salvation. That is why Paul tells them he did not come, "in cleverness of speech, so that the cross of Christ would not be made void" (1 Cor. 1.17). Regardless of their present fascination with "cleverness of speech" (an allusion to worldly wisdom in keeping with the cultural milieu of the day), Paul was unmoved by their flirtatious fascination with the world's false forms of diverse knowledge:

> "Fascinated by the rhetoric of learned scholars of their day, the Corinthians were sometimes more impressed by form and show than by content and truth. They loved "words of human wisdom" (1:17)— literally, "wisdom of word," the wit and eloquence that neatly packaged more than one school of thought in first-century Greece."[170]

Regardless of what people seem to be gravitating towards, pastors today can have the same Pauline assurance that in preaching the message of the cross, they are fulfilling what God has called them to do (1 Cor. 4.1; 2 Tim. 2.2). They do not need to add to their preaching other techniques for communicating God's message. They do not need to intersperse their sermons with their personalities, jokes, and shallow stories. They do not need to present endless programs for felt needs, the way a waiter runs through a menu in order to get God's people interested in God—they simply need to be faithful to the ministry of the Word and preach it in the power of the Spirit (1 Cor. 4.2). It is remarkable to have to write, but even more remarkable that some ministers are not yet awake to the fact that the primary task that God has for preachers is—*preaching*! More than organizing, more than counseling, more than church planting, more than administration, more than networking; nothing can replace the primacy and sufficiency of preaching Christ in all of His preeminent glory (Col. 1.18). Oh, that every Christian minister could say with Paul the following autobiographical declaration without fear of congregational backlash:

Colossians 1:25–29 [25] "Of this church I was made a minister according to the stewardship from God bestowed on me for your benefit, so that I might fully carry out the preaching of the word

---

[170]Carson, *The Cross and Christian Ministry*, p.13.

of God, [26] that is, the mystery which has been hidden from the past ages and generations, but has now been manifested to His saints, [27] to whom God willed to make known what is the riches of the glory of this mystery among the Gentiles, which is Christ in you, the hope of glory. [28] We proclaim Him, admonishing every man and teaching every man with all wisdom, so that we may present every man complete in Christ. [29] For this purpose also I labor, striving according to His power, which mightily works within me."

The only fear that Paul had is expressed in the latter part of v.17, "For Christ did not send me to baptize, but to preach the gospel, not in cleverness of speech, *so that the cross of Christ would not be made void.*" Fill the message of Christianity with manmade wisdom and you empty the cross of its power. This "cleverness of speech", which Paul speaks of here, needs to be carefully defined before moving on. *Paul is referring to sensational orators who were rooted in the philosophy of human reason, and driven by rhetorical techniques taken from the culture, that were aimed at drawing a following based, not on substance, but style, personality and delivery.* Paul will branch out from here to take aim directly at "the wisdom of the world" as that which is contrary to God's wisdom supremely displayed in the cross (cf. 1 Cor. 1.20). Paul's fear was that the Corinthians were substituting the power of God for what possessed no power at all simply because of its rhetorical or philosophical appeal. Making the cross *void*[171] refers to the potential of losing the efficacy of the gospel by distorting the primitive message of the cross with what is falsely perceived to be more appealing, palatable and relevant for one's own cultural context.

The Wisdom of God Displayed On The Cross

1 Corinthians 1:18 [18] "For the word of the cross is foolishness to those who are perishing, but to us who are being saved it is the power of God."

We should also point out that part of Paul's context in Corinth was the Jew/Gentile world that made up Paul's entire socio-economic and spiritual climate within the dominance of a Greco-Roman empire. What these two categories of people had in common, however, was that, apart

---

[171] κενόω. The word literally means to render something without result or effect (see, BDAG).

from the gospel, their wisdom was reduced to foolishness. From the divine perspective, the cross grants a person access to the wisdom of God. From the perspective of fallen humanity, whether Jew or Gentile, the cross was the epitome of foolishness. These are, therefore, two worldviews in collision. Two diametrically opposed worldviews and philosophies on life itself. As some have commented, "the cross signals the end of human wisdom."[172] Despite the many kinds of divisions that existed in Paul's day down to our very own day; the cross brings in the ultimate dividing line:

> "Paul asserts that *the message of the cross* divides the race: it constitutes *foolishness* to some, but *power* to others. The ancient world was familiar with a number of radical polarities: people were either Roman or barbarian, Jew or Gentile, slave or free, male or female. Society was anything but equal and classless. However, *the cross* renders all of these divisions redundant and obsolete. The only separation that counts is between those who are *perishing* and those who are *being saved*".[173]

Paul makes it clear that "the word of the cross"[174] has ushered, not only, the end of the world's wisdom, but also, a hostile sword of division between those who are perishing and those who are being saved (cf. 2 Cor. 6.14-16), so that there is now an "implacable opposition between human wisdom and the word of the cross."[175]

1 Corinthians 1:18 [18] "For the word of the cross is foolishness to those who are perishing, but to us who are being saved it is the power of God."

---

[172]Roy E. Ciampa and Brian S. Rosner, *The First Letter to the Corinthians*, The Pillar New Testament Commentary (Grand Rapids, MI; Cambridge, U.K.: William B. Eerdmans Publishing Company, 2010), 90.

[173]Ibid.

[174]Greek: Ὁ λόγος γὰρ ὁ τοῦ σταυροῦ. In the context, this phrase has a close assoiciation not with the abstract idea of a "message", as in, "the message of the cross", but rather, something more akin to "the preaching of the cross" or "the proclamation of the cross." Evidence can be found in the parallel of 1 Cor. 1.17 "cleverness of speech" (literally, "wisdom of word" or "word's wisdom", σοφία λόγου); also the "preaching" (κήρυγμα) of v.21 and the "proclaiming" (καταγγέλλω) or 1 Cor. 2.2. Also see, "Anthony C. Thiselton, *The First Epistle to the Corinthians: a Commentary on the Greek Text*, New International Greek Testament Commentary (Grand Rapids, MI: W.B. Eerdmans, 2000), 153-154.

[175]G. K. Beale and D. A. Carson, *Commentary on the New Testament Use of the Old Testament* (Grand Rapids, MI; Nottingham, UK: Baker Academic; Apollos, 2007), 697.

As Paul saw it, God's very power was revealed through the *weakness* of the cross that was preached and proclaimed in Paul's ministry (1 Cor. 1.27).[176] The reality is that the cross actually reveals just how weak and impotent people are to arrive at divine knowledge. *The cross is the soul of the gospel because it brings us to the very soul and mind of God.* Centuries of philosophers, historians, pagans, diviners, sorcerers, false prophets, wise men, and free thinkers could not achieve with all of their collective efforts and *wisdom*—supported by rulers, kings, powers and authorities of vast dynasties and empires—that which God did through the old rugged cross; that is, bring mankind into the knowledge of God:

> **1 Corinthians 1:21** [21] "For since in the wisdom of God the world through its wisdom did not come to know God, God was well-pleased through the foolishness of the message preached to save those who believe."

The cross was God's instrument for destroying the "wisdom of the wise" (1 Cor. 1.19). Through the cross, the "cleverness of the clever" has been "set aside." The fact that Paul is quoting from Isaiah 29.14 also says two additional things about the way Paul wanted us to understand his emphasis on the cross and God's wisdom. *First*, the text is leveled at the foolish counselors of King Hezekiah at the time. By this implication, Paul is saying that the wisdom of earthly rulers, God has "set aside" (1 Cor. 1.19b). So Pilate, Caesar, Herod, and the United Nations, etc., all the nations and their rulers and political structures have had their *wisdom* decimated by the cross of God's anointed Son-King (Psalm 2). It has rendered the wisdom of the rulers of this age impotent for knowing God and understanding the mind of God. Paul will go on to say, "if they had understood it [God's wisdom] they would not have crucified the Lord of glory" (1 Cor. 2.8b).

Second, the text is also redemptive-historical in focus, in that, what may have been perceived as a failure on God's part by allowing His people to fall to Assyria was actually the display of God's redemptive power and wisdom ultimately to be revealed in Christ. The entire passage is helpful here:

> **Isaiah 29:14** [14] "Therefore behold, I will once again deal marvelously with this people, wondrously marvelous; And the wisdom

---

[176]Of course, by extension this now applies to the Church in general.

of their wise men will perish, And the discernment of their discerning men will be concealed."

This suits the context of Paul's argument perfectly. To the Jews, the very notion of a crucified Messiah was repulsive and unthinkable (cf. Jn. 12.34; Gal. 3.10; Dt. 21.23). Likewise, to the Greek mind, the idea that God would become a man and take on *flesh* for the purpose of dying and rising again was also nonsense as far as they were concerned (Acts 17). Yet, this paradoxical cross is precisely what God was referring to when He spoke of dealing "marvelously with this people, wondrously marvelous." Earlier the prophet spoke of God's "task, His unusual task… His work, His extraordinary work" (Is. 28.21-22). Paul sees the "wondrously marvelous", "extraordinary work" fulfilled in redemption's apex—the cross![177] It is the cross that so many today, sadly, still consider to be only foolishness.

I recall watching a debate between James White and Adnan Rashid regarding whether or not Jesus and Muhammad preached the same message. During a question and answer period in the debate, Adnan Rashid insisted that the Christian message made no sense to him, asking the students at Trinity College in Dublin, "What kind of God would send His son to slay Him on a cross?… God is merciful!" But this is precisely the point, "the message of the cross is foolishness" to the two billion Muslims who are perishing without the cross, precisely because they fail to see the extraordinary mercy of the cross. The issue was no different in Paul's own day. Both Jews and Gentiles regarded the cross as nothing. But as Paul went on to demonstrate, the cross paradoxically turns the tables on what some perceive to be reality when it is not:

> **1 Corinthians 1:22–31** [22] "For indeed Jews ask for signs and Greeks search for wisdom; [23] but we preach Christ crucified, to Jews a stumbling block and to Gentiles foolishness, [24] but to those who are the called, both Jews and Greeks, Christ the power of God and the wisdom of God. [25] Because the foolishness

---

[177]The eschatological conclusion drawn at v.22 only adds to its redemptive-historical Messianic fulfillment, "For I have heard from the Lord God of hosts of decisive destruction on all the earth." Also see, Rom. 10.11-13. Beale sees this passage as referring to the church as "The Transformed and Restored Eschatological Israel"; G. K. Beale, *A New Testament Biblical Theology: The Unfolding of the Old Testament in the New* (Grand Rapids, MI: Baker Academic, 2011), 709

of God is wiser than men, and the weakness of God is stronger than men. [26] For consider your calling, brethren, that there were not many wise according to the flesh, not many mighty, not many noble; [27] but God has chosen the foolish things of the world to shame the wise, and God has chosen the weak things of the world to shame the things which are strong, [28] and the base things of the world and the despised God has chosen, the things that are not, so that He may nullify the things that are, [29] so that no man may boast before God. [30] But by His doing you are in Christ Jesus, who became to us wisdom from God, and righteousness and sanctification, and redemption, [31] so that, just as it is written, "Let him who boasts, boast in the Lord."

The Power of God And The Proclamation of The Cross

1 Corinthians 2:1–5 [1] "And when I came to you, brethren, I did not come with superiority of speech or of wisdom, proclaiming to you the testimony of God. [2] For I determined to know nothing among you except Jesus Christ, and Him crucified. [3] I was with you in weakness and in fear and in much trembling, [4] and my message and my preaching were not in persuasive words of wisdom, but in demonstration of the Spirit and of power, [5] so that your faith would not rest on the wisdom of men, but on the power of God."

Again, returning for a moment to the oratory backdrop of 1 Corinthians 1-2, verses 1-5 of the first chapter are somewhat of an expanded version of (1 Cor. 1.17), for it teaches us that God's power is found not in "cleverness of speech", but again in the proclamation about Jesus Christ and Him crucified. But the clever speech of the ancient sophists was driven by the need to appease their audience through adaptation to culture and contextualizing their message to meet the demands of the listening mobs. Carson illuminates the ancient background:

"It has been persuasively argued that Paul is alluding to the sophist of his day. Many intellectual movements greatly prized rhetoric. Philosophers were as widely praised for their oratory as for their content. But the sophists brought these ideals to new heights. Following fairly rigid and somewhat artificial conventions, these public speakers were praised and followed (and gained paying students!) in proportion to their ability to declaim in public assembly, to choose a theme and expatiate on it with telling power, and to speak convincingly and movingly in legal, religious, business, and political contexts. They enjoyed such widespread influence in the Mediterranean world, not least in Corinth, that public speakers who either could not meet their standards, or who for any reason chose no to, were viewed as seriously inferior."[178]

But Paul renounced all such ulterior motives for preaching. Too many pastors today are still attempting this cultural adaptation in their preaching. In reality, the cross is not just unpopular with popular culture; it is counter-cultural. It flies directly in the face of the world's *wisdom*. This is why Paul refused to delude the message of the cross with cultural additives; they were unsound preservatives with no real spiritual nutritional value. He later would tell the Corinthians:

> **2 Corinthians 4:1–2** [1] "Therefore, since we have this ministry, as we received mercy, we do not lose heart, [2] but we have renounced the things hidden because of shame, not walking in craftiness or adulterating the word of God, but by the manifestation of truth commending ourselves to every man's conscience in the sight of God."

This is why Paul, unlike the sophists of Corinth, could not be bought. Paul's resolution to preach Christ crucified is, at one and the same time, a decision to preach God's Word uncompromisingly, unapologetically, and unashamedly; and also to resist the temptation to preach anything else. Paul did what Carson calls preachers to today when he says, "When the pressure to 'contextualize' the gospel jeopardizes the message of the cross by inflating human egos, the cultural pressures must be ignored."[179] So Paul says, "I determined to know nothing among you except Jesus Christ, and Him crucified." For the apostle Paul, this resolve was the only proper way of building on a good foundation (1 Cor. 3.10-11), it was the only kind of substance that would withstand God's final assize (1 Cor. 3.13), and it was the only thing that possessed true philosophical and, more importantly, spiritual power (1 Cor. 1.18).

---

[178]Carson, The Cross and Christian Ministry, 33-34.

[179]Ibid, 34.

Paul's Cross-Centered Resolve Is Rooted In God's Church

Paul's cross-centered resolve was also rooted in his theology of the church. Paul saw the abiding benefits of the gospel for the church. Not only does the cross ensure that the church's faith will be built on God's power and not on man's impotent sophistry (1 Cor. 2.4-5), it also ensures the church's edification in true wisdom and knowledge (cf. Col. 3.10). This is seen in at least three ways. *First, the wisdom of God has been fore-ordained for the Church*:

> **1 Corinthians 2:6–9** [6] "Yet we do speak wisdom among those who are mature; a wisdom, however, not of this age nor of the rulers of this age, who are passing away; [7] but we speak God's wisdom in a mystery, the hidden wisdom which God predestined before the ages to our glory; [8] the wisdom which none of the rulers of this age has understood; for if they had understood it they would not have crucified the Lord of glory; [9] but just as it is written, "Things which eye has not seen and ear has not heard, And which have not entered the heart of man, All that God has prepared for those who love Him.""

The cross reminds us that God's plan of redemption through Jesus Christ was part of God's eternal decree that would result in our everlasting good (cf. Jer. 32.40-41; Lk. 12.42; Rev. 21.1-4). Paul gives a parallel in Ephesians:

> **Ephesians 3:8–11** [8] "To me, the very least of all saints, this grace was given, to preach to the Gentiles the unfathomable riches of Christ, [9] and to bring to light what is the administration of the mystery which for ages has been hidden in God who created all things; [10] so that the manifold wisdom of God might now be made known through the church to the rulers and the authorities in the heavenly places. [11] This was in accordance with the eternal purpose which He carried out in Christ Jesus our Lord..."

God's eternal purpose was that the crosswork of Christ would, not only procure God's elect, but would also *bless* God's elect with every spiritual blessing in Christ (Eph. 1.3-4). The language of predestination should not surprise us here. As Hodge has pointed out,

"The idea that the scheme of redemption, which the apostle here calls the wisdom of God, was from eternity formed in the divine mind, far out of the reach of human penetration, and has under the gospel been made known for the salvation of men, is one often presented by the apostle."[180]

Many Christians have come to see Paul's use of Isaiah 64 and 65 in purely eschatological terms, thinking the things God has *prepared* refer only to heaven.[181] But in the context of Isaiah 64 the prophet is thinking mainly of how God is going to remove the sin of the people. This is why Isaiah, personifying the people of Israel, deals directly with the people's state of spiritual demise:

> **Isaiah 64:5–7** [5] "You meet him who rejoices in doing righteousness, Who remembers You in Your ways. Behold, You were angry, for we sinned, We continued in them a long time; And shall we be saved? [6] For all of us have become like one who is unclean, And all our righteous deeds are like a filthy garment; And all of us wither like a leaf, And our iniquities, like the wind, take us away. [7] There is no one who calls on Your name, Who arouses himself to take hold of You; For You have hidden Your face from us And have delivered us into the power of our iniquities."

What Paul saw in Isaiah's work, what God had *prepared*, what "eye has not seen, and ear has not heard", was the redemptive crosswork of Christ in delivering God's people from their sins. As Paul saw it, the cross was the answer to the people's lack of righteousness, their ongoing sin, their uncleanness, their filth, their iniquities, and apathy in seeking the Lord. Paul was resolved to preach Christ crucified because this redemptive work was what God had foreordained for the church's good, as Calvin put it, "that we might enjoy it."[182] It did not enter into "the heart of man" because the redemptive work of the cross is not human in origin and could never arise from man's natural mind for it is actually contrary to it (cf. 1 Cor. 1.18). It is rooted instead in the bowels of divine wisdom

---

[180]Charles Hodge, *A Commentary of 1 & 2 Corinthians: Geneva Series of Commentaries* (Edinburgh/Carlisle: Banner of Truth, 2000) 35-36.

[181]See, John MacArthur, *1 Corinthians* (1984) 61.

[182]John Calvin, *Calvin Commentaries:* Vol. XX (Grand Rapids: Baker, 2005) 104.

and foreordained for our good (cf. 1 Cor. 3.18).[183] This same emphasis on God's sovereign plan regarding the cross can be seen from the earliest prayers of the church:[184]

> **Acts 4:24–28** [24] "And when they heard this, they lifted their voices to God with one accord and said, "O Lord, it is You who made the heaven and the earth and the sea, and all that is in them, [25] who by the Holy Spirit, through the mouth of our father David Your servant, said, 'Why did the Gentiles rage, And the peoples devise futile things? [26] 'The kings of the earth took their stand, And the rulers were gathered together Against the Lord and against His Christ.' [27] "For truly in this city there were gathered together against Your holy servant Jesus, whom You anointed, both Herod and Pontius Pilate, along with the Gentiles and the peoples of Israel, [28] to do whatever Your hand and Your purpose predestined to occur."

Second, there is also a *pneumatological* component to Paul's resolve. God's Spirit is also the Revealer of God's wisdom. Paul was resolved to preach Christ crucified because, *the wisdom of God has been revealed through the Spirit to the Church*:

> **1 Corinthians 2:10–13** [10] "For to us God revealed them through the Spirit; for the Spirit searches all things, even the depths of God. [11] For who among men knows the thoughts of a man except the spirit of the man which is in him? Even so the thoughts of God no one knows except the Spirit of God. [12] Now we have received, not the spirit of the world, but the Spirit who is from God, so that we may know the things freely given to us by God, [13] which things we also speak, not in words taught by human wisdom, but in those taught by the Spirit, combining spiritual thoughts with spiritual words."

---

[183]As to the use of Isaiah 64 & 65 in 1 Corinthians 2.9 see, Beale, G. K., and D. A. Carson. *Commentary on the New Testament Use of the Old Testament*. (Grand Rapids, MI; Nottingham, UK: Baker Academic; Apollos, 2007) 701.

[184]From a redemptive-historical perspective, the element of sovereignty is only heightened by the utilization of these OT texts (Ps. 146.6; Ps. 2.1-2: the use of Ps. 2 is an exact quote from the LXX); demonstrating the prophetic future signifying of the Old Testament with regard to the cross.

Paul moves away from simply asserting that God has chosen to reveal the mystery of the cross to us and explains *how* He does this, namely through the Spirit. Paul's analogy that only the spirit within the man knows the thoughts of the man illustrates that God's wisdom cannot be understood or appropriated apart from the life-giving, wisdom-imparting activity of the Spirit of God. Since the Spirit knows God's thoughts best, He is uniquely qualified to reveal them to us. But what the Spirit is revealing are not random thoughts known by God, but precisely the nature of salvation as found in the crosswork of Jesus Christ. The Son's redemptive work, becomes the content of the Spirit's redemptive revelation to His people (cf. 1 Jn. 2.26-27).

The purpose of preaching the *cross* and not preaching moralism, legalism, theories, opinions, economics, politics and mere spirituality is done in the hope that God will perform this miracle of understanding His mystery of the cross. The hope is that as the Spirit is pleased to blow wherever He wills, a supernatural illumination might be given and the wisdom of God, concerning a scandalous cross, revealed to the darkened minds of sinners (John 3.5-8). That's why we do not try to manipulate people with words of human wisdom (e.g. psychology) in the attempt to produce external change. If people are to respond to the gospel, they must respond to the power of the cross or else it is not God enabling them to respond, but instead, it is self. The Corinthians were too impressed with rhetorical devices that sought to impress people by the relevance and appeal of a clever message. But the cross is a message that flies in the face of man's carnal expectations and selfish demands (cf. 1 Cor. 1.22). The cross is contrary to the mind of man in general (cf. Rom. 8.7-9). Paul understood the necessity for the Spirit's work in his preaching—without God the Spirit brining this illumination, the carnal mind of the sinner would manufacture a response by the power of the flesh and the empty wisdom of man and not the wisdom of God through the preaching of the cross taught by the Spirit of the living God (cf. 2 Cor. 7.10). This is what Paul means in saying, [12] "Now we have received, not the spirit of the world, but the Spirit who is from God, so that we may know the things freely given to us by God, [13] which things we also speak, not in words taught by human wisdom, but in those taught by the Spirit" (1 Cor. 2.12-13).

Before moving on to the final point, we should not miss the blatant Trinitarian structure of this passage. A simple outline brings this out: The

Son accomplishes the redemption of the cross (1 Cor. 2.1-5), the *Father* is credited with decreeing redemption for His Church (1 Cor. 2.6-9), and the *Spirit* is credited with revealing the nature of redemption by revealing God's thoughts and the mind of Christ to the Church (1 Cor. 2.10-16). When the cross-work of Jesus is seen from this Trinitarian panoramic, we see that the work of the cross redounds to the glory of God (see also, Eph. 1.3-14).[185]

Third, Paul was also resolved to preach Christ crucified because he possessed the mind of Christ. That is to say, *the wisdom of God has been revealed to the Church through the mind of Christ*:

> **1 Corinthians 2:14–16** [14] "But a natural man does not accept the things of the Spirit of God, for they are foolishness to him; and he cannot understand them, because they are spiritually appraised. [15] But he who is spiritual appraises all things, yet he himself is appraised by no one. [16] For who has known the mind of the Lord, that he will instruct Him? But we have the mind of Christ."

The phrase "the mind of Christ" has to do with possessing God's hidden wisdom through the impartation of the mind of Christ to His people, "we have the mind of Christ." When Paul appeals to the Philippians to live and dwell in unity, he appeals to them as those who possess the mind of Christ and thus should live like it (Phil. 2.5). It means to think *like* Christ thinks. The reason that the unbeliever does not have the ability to understand the gospel and the wisdom and power of the cross, is because he does not have the right "mind." But that is not to say that they simply lack more of what is already in their minds, like a higher IQ versus a lower IQ, but rather, they lack a different mind altogether. The problem is not so much functional, as it is ontological. They do not simply lack information, but istead, they lack *illumination*. Remarkably, the cross of Christ can only be truly understood with the *mind* of Christ.

The maddening reality of this, is that man in his sinful condition will always regard the glory, power, beauty, love, grace and wisdom of

---

[185]The same basic structure is found in Ephesians as the Father chooses and determines the objects of salvation (Eph. 1.3-6), the Son accomplishes salvation (Eph. 1.7-12), and the Spirit applies redemption in harmony with God's choice and the Son's redemptive work on the cross (Eph. 1.13-14).

God, displayed on the cross, as "foolishness", "But a natural man does not accept the things of the Spirit of God, for they are foolishness to him; and he cannot understand them, because they are spiritually appraised" (v.14). Without the mind of Christ, a person will never be able to *appraise* either the wisdom of the cross, nor those who preach it, for we are in fact *un-appraisable*. As one commentary put it, "The spiritual person is not ultimately subject to merely human judgments since, as the end of v. 14 indicates, spiritual things (and spiritual people) are understood only via the Spirit, which the things/people of the world lack."[186]

Preaching the cross brings out these epistemic dimensions. The "mind of Christ" is a worldview as much as it is a mystical/spiritual condition. Remarkably, many in the Church today labor to make the cross subject to *merely human judgment* assuming sinners devoid of salvation can rightly appraise the "things of the Spirit of God", they cannot. God delights to bring sinners to himself through the foolishness of the message preached (cf. 1 Cor. 1.21). The reason for this is so that our faith would rest in God's power and not human wisdom. There may also be another important component here. Without God's grace, His Spirit, and His mind, the natural man tends towards viewing salvation in an *autosoteric* fashion. Hearing what they want to hear, the natural man thinks of salvation as something man can earn or produce through human effort and not by grace. Grace is central to the preaching of the cross because it iswhat the cross is all about, " " (2.12). Here is what the wisdom of the world will never understand apart from God's Spirit and grace; what they lack they do not posses and what they need they cannot earn because salvation is "freely given to us by God."[187]

Paul says as Christians "we have the mind of Christ" (1 Cor. 2.16), and as such, we have come to know the wisdom of God's message of the cross. Because we have the mind of Christ, our message is rather simple however profound, 'the cross is man's only hope, but in order for sinners to avert eternal destruction, they must be willing to become fools for

---

[186]Roy E. Ciampa and Brian S. Rosner, *The First Letter to the Corinthians*, 137.

[187]Gk: ἵνα εἰδῶμεν τὰ ὑπὸ τοῦ θεοῦ χαρισθέντα ἡμῖν. The purpose of the Spirit's work is epistemic, "to know", but the content of that knowledge indicates two other things. *First*, that salvation is "free" and therefore cannot be earned in any way (Eph. 2.8). *Second*, that salvation is imparted by *God*, not ourselves or any other source of wisdom man can contrive. It also suggests that what God has in fact sovereignly given by His grace is found only in the cross.

Christ's sake (by turning from all self-reliance and trusting solely in the Lord of Glory Himself Jesus Christ who was crucified and rose again on behalf of those who would repent and believe), everything else as God sees it, is true foolishness.

Like Paul, our churches, if they are to be true churches, must never grow past the scandal of the cross (1 Cor. 1.23-24). We must never think to leave behind that which the world regards as foolish for that which the world regards as wisdom, which is no wisdom at all. Only through the preaching of Christ crucified will we be in line with God's mandate to Paul and by extension to the church for all ages. Only through the gospel will we truly find the wisdom and power that people so desperately need. Only the cross can produce a sufficient foundation for our faith. It is only the preaching of the cross that the Spirit delights to bless and through the cross impart the very wisdom of God by giving us the mind of the very One who was sent to die so that we may live.

Solus Christus

Made in the USA
Coppell, TX
04 February 2021

49447895R00095